Mastering Computer Typing

REVISED EDITION

Mastering Computer Typing

REVISED EDITION

Sheryl Lindsell-Roberts

Houghton Mifflin Harcourt
Boston   New York

Visit our website: www.hmhbooks.com

Library of Congress Cataloging-in-Publication Data

Lindsell-Roberts, Sheryl.
  Mastering computer typing / Sheryl Lindsell-Roberts. — Rev. ed.
    p. cm.
  ISBN-13: 978-0-547-33319-9 (alk. paper)
  ISBN-10: 0-547-33319-6 (alk. paper)
  1. Electronic data processing — Keyboarding.   I. Title.
  QA76.9.K48L57 2010
652.3—dc22

                                              2009026747

Manufactured in the United States of America

Book design by Publishers' Design and Production Services, Inc.

1 2 3 4 5 6 7 8 9 10-MER-15 14 13 12 11 10

Microsoft Word, Excel, and PowerPoint are registered trademarks of Microsoft Corporation.

Contents

PART THREE   PRACTICAL APPLICATIONS

APPENDIXES

PART ONE

Introduction

GETTING STARTED

Who Needs to Type?

You do! Whether you're a student, secretary, office administrator, manager, computer programmer, attorney, CPA, scientist, or engineer, typing is an invaluable skill. It's a skill that can open doors and enhance your career opportunities. In this high-tech world of computer-generated communications (emails, blogs, texting, instant messaging, social networking, word processing, networks, bulletin boards, and much more), anyone who can't type runs the risk of being excluded from many business and social transactions.

About This Book

This book is designed for self-instruction or classroom instruction. You'll be guided through each module, or unit of instruction, in a sequential and logical manner and will join millions of typists who have become proficient through this step-by-step method of learning to type. You'll begin your development by typing simple words and proceed through a wide array of practical applications.

The book is divided into four sections, each with a different purpose.

1. The *Introduction* includes information on hardware and software, computer applications and procedures, and ways to avoid office aches and pains.
2. *Learning to Type* acquaints you with the keyboard through numerous practice exercises.
3. *Practical Applications* presents real-world business applications for using a computer, including charts, letters, manuscripts, and business-related exercises.
4. The *Appendixes* contain a variety of timed typings you can use as you progress through the book, a glossary of computer terms, and a guide to punctuation.

Picture Credits

Publishers' Design & Production Services, Inc.: illustrations on pages 2, 13, 19, 26, 34, 43, 54, 111, and 157

Courtesy of abKey® Pte Ltd.: abKey® Next Generation keyboard on page 3

Courtesy of SafeType, Inc.: Safetype™ keyboard on page 3

Courtesy of P.C.D. Maltron Ltd. at www.maltron.com: Maltron Single-Handed keyboard on page 3

Courtesy of Bitstream Inc. and Microsoft Corporation: Wingdings screenshot on page 5

Courtesy of Microsoft Corporation: screenshots on page 6

Courtesy of Office Star Products, Ontario, California: Office Star 3680 mid-back executive chair on page 9

Fotosearch.com, photo by SassyStock: wrist rest photograph on page 11

Catherine Hawkes, Cat & Mouse: Proofreaders' Marks table on page 147

"Brain Busters" are included in each module. They are not meant to measure your intelligence, clean up the environment, or pay off the national debt. They are intended to give you something to think about while having, I hope, a little fun.

Your Objective

Your primary objective should be to touch-type; that is, to type without looking at the keyboard or your fingers. If you turn your head back and forth between the keyboard and the copy, you will not only give yourself a stiff neck but will also slow down, make errors, and lose your place.

Although this book can teach you to type in 24 hours, each person learns at a different pace. Your progress will depend on your past typing experiences and your determination.

KNOW YOUR KEYBOARD

Get to know your computer keyboard. Refer to the Help menu or the instruction manual that accompanies your hardware if you have any questions.

A standardized "QWERTY" keyboard will be found on most computers and word processors. If you look at the top row of letters, you will notice the QWERTY sequence. All alphabetical keys and numbers will appear in the same place no matter what computer you're using. Some symbols, punctuation marks, or special keys may differ from one keyboard to another and some enhanced keyboards may include a second set of function keys and other special or duplicate keys, so you should always check the location of the special keys on the keyboard you're using.

QWERTY keyboard

#15: Traumatic Tales

1. The Wizard of Oz
2. Jack Sprat
3. Jack and the Beanstalk
4. Tom Sawyer
5. Humpty Dumpty
6. The Owl and the Pussycat
7. Goldilocks and the Three Bears
8. Cinderella
9. Snow White
10. Little Bo Peep

Fixed or split?

Inventors have created a variety of keyboards to make typing faster and to address the debilitating pain many people suffer in their arms and wrists, often known as carpal tunnel syndrome.

The most popular are the fixed-split and adjustable-split keyboards (such as the abKey® Next Generation keyboard by abKey®, below). It splits into two pieces so the user can change the angle for maximum comfort, and the most common letters in the alphabet are in or near the home row.

Weird or what?

Not all keyboards are QWERTY; some are QUIRKY (such as the Safetype™ keyboard by SafeType, Inc., and the Maltron Single-Handed keyboard by P.C.D. Maltron Ltd., pictured below). Some people see them as a blessing; others see them as just plain weird. Form your own opinion.

#12: Hyperboles, Metaphors, Similes, and Clichés

1. raining cats and dogs
2. so hungry I could eat a horse
3. eating us out of house and home
4. as old as Methuselah
5. busy as a one-armed paper hanger; busy as a bee
6. talk one's ears off
7. so mad I could spit nails
8. driving like a bat out of hell
9. know the place like the back of my hand
10. take a bath

#13: Goof-Proof

1. Some say **never to split** an infinitive.
2. A verb should agree with **its** subject.
3. Proofread carefully to see if words **were** left out **or** repeated.
4. A writer shouldn't shift **his or her** point of view.
5. If any word is **im**proper at the end of a sentence, **it is** a linking verb.
6. Take the bull by the **horns** and never mix metaphors.
7. Always **pick the** correct idiom.
8. In general, a preposition isn't a word **with which** you should end a sentence.
9. **Consider** shortening long sentences **by deleting** unnecessary words.
10. **Avoid clichés.**

#14: Simply Stated

1. Like father, like son.
2. People in glass houses shouldn't throw stones.
3. Beggars can't be choosers.
4. Don't cry over spilled milk.
5. Beauty is only skin-deep.
6. All that glitters is not gold.
7. Honesty is the best policy.
8. United we stand; divided we fall.
9. You can't judge a book by its cover.
10. A bird in the hand is worth two in the bush.

FONTS

Monospacing vs. Proportional Spacing

In a monospaced font, every character takes up the same amount of horizontal space. In a proportional font, the amount of space the character takes up is proportional to its width. For example, the letter *m* takes up more space than the letter *i*. Proportional fonts are often easier to read, but monospaced fonts are best for some purposes, such as computer programming, because the letters align in neat columns. On a computer you have the option of using letters that are monospaced or proportionally spaced.

```
This is an example of monospacing. All the letters are
evenly spaced.
```

This is an example of proportional spacing. The letters are spaced according to size.

Note

All the exercises in this book are shown in a monospaced 12-point font. If you're using a different font, your output will not match the book line for line. That's OK.

Font Styles

This is an example of serif type called Times Roman, which has little finishing lines on the letters.

This is an example of sans serif type called Arial, which has no little finishing lines on the letters.

This is an example of italic.

This is an example of bold.

#9: Who's Afraid?

1. claustrophobia
2. agoraphobia
3. aquaphobia
4. xenophobia
5. verbophobia
6. hematophobia
7. acrophobia
8. nyctophobia
9. gamophobia
10. arachibutyrophobia

#10: Red, White, and Blue

1. blackmail
2. talks a blue streak
3. yellow-bellied
4. red-carpet treatment
5. give the green light
6. tickled pink
7. in the limelight
8. brown-bag it
9. whitewash
10. wearing rose-colored glasses

#11: Seascapes

1. runs a tight ship
2. bailout
3. from stem to stern
4. harbor a grudge
5. Hit the deck!
6. Don't rock the boat.
7. all washed up
8. give leeway
9. steer clear of
10. between the devil and the deep blue sea

THIS IS AN EXAMPLE OF SMALL CAPS.

Font Sizes   This is 8 point Times Roman.

This is 10 point Times Roman.

This is 12 point Times Roman.

This is 18 point Times Roman.

This is 24 point Times Roman.

Note   A serif font, such as Times Roman, is recommended for hard copy and a sans serif font, such as Arial, is recommended for electronic copy.

SYMBOLS AND SPECIAL CHARACTERS

In addition to a wide variety of font selections, you can select symbols and special characters. In Microsoft Word, you find them by pulling down the Insert menu and clicking on Symbols. Here's a smattering of what you can use:

Wingdings

#6: Letter Perfect

1. 26 = letters in the alphabet
2. 1,001 = Arabian Nights
3. 12 = signs of the zodiac
4. 5,280 = feet in a mile
5. 88 = keys on a piano
6. 13 = stripes on the American flag
7. 32 = degrees at which water freezes
8. 90 = degrees in a right angle
9. 8 = sides on a stop sign
10. 4 = quarts in a gallon

#7: Beastasaurus Rex

1. night owls
2. fighting like cats and dogs
3. play possum
4. pigheaded
5. no spring chicken
6. talk turkey
7. guinea pig
8. straw that broke the camel's back
9. can of worms
10. goose that laid the golden egg

#8: Foodaholic

1. nuts; bananas
2. in a jam; in a pickle
3. lemon
4. butter up
5. long drink of water
6. bowl of cherries
7. slow as molasses
8. piece of cake; easy as pie
9. that's the way the cookie crumbles
10. carrot-top

Special characters

	Symbol	
	Symbols Special Characters	

Character: **Shortcut key:**

—	Em Dash	Command+Option+Numpad–
–	En Dash	Command+Numpad–
‑	Nonbreaking Hyphen	Command+Shift+‑
	Optional Hyphen	Command+‑
	Em Space	
	En Space	
~	Nonbreaking Space	Control+Shift+Space Bar
©	Copyright	Option+G
®	Registered	Option+R
™	Trademark	Option+2
§	Section	Option+6
¶	Paragraph	Option+7
…	Ellipsis	Option+;

(AutoCorrect...)   (Shortcut Key...)

(Cancel)   (Insert)

Characters for foreign words

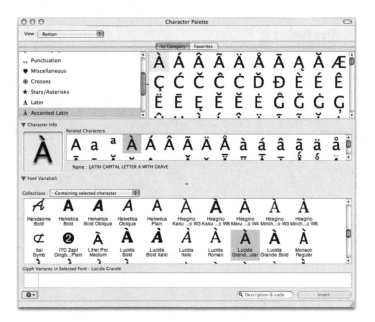

Symbols and Special Characters

Brain Buster Answers

#1: QWERTY

1. typewriter
2. proprietor
3. perpetuity

#2: 28-Letter Word

antidisestablishmentarianism

#3: Three Consecutive Double Letters

b**ookkee**ping *or* b**ookkee**per

#4: Consecutive Vowels

1. seeing
2. sequoia
3. queueing

#5: Oxymorons

1. live
2. opposition
3. deviation
4. justice
5. teacher
6. silverware
7. order
8. ugly
9. War
10. news

JUSTIFICATION

On a computer you can select various justifications (or alignments).

Left Justify

> Everything aligns to the left. This is a very popular style for letters.

Full Justify or Justify

> Many of us are used to seeing this type of justification in books and publications. When you use this type of justification, be careful you do not create unusual spacing between words that can cause rivers (streaks of white space) that flow down the page.

Center Justify

> Everything is centered. This is a popular style for headings, invitations, announcements, etc.

Right Justify

> All your text appears at the right. This is generally reserved for special circumstances such as invitations, announcements, etc.

BORDERS AND RULES

Here are some examples of what you can create on a computer.

Single-Border Box

> This is an example of a single-border box.

Double-Border Box

> This is an example of a double-border box.

QUOTATION MARKS

Note   Commas and periods always go inside quotation marks. Colons and semicolons always go outside quotation marks. Question marks and exclamation points go inside quotation marks when they apply to the quoted material only. They go outside when they apply to the entire sentence. For example:

> She asked, "Did you finish the English course?"

> Why did you call that task "impossible"?

- To surround something or someone being directly quoted (exact words):

> "I like your idea," Mr. James commented.

- To enclose titles of articles, short poems, lectures or topics, paintings, short stories, or chapters:

> In THE SECRETARY'S QUICK REFERENCE HANDBOOK there's a chapter entitled "Desktop Publishing."

- To set off words or phrases introduced by an expression such as *the word*, *known as*, *called*, etc.

> The check was marked "canceled."

- To set off words that are used in an unconventional manner:

> He is "hot stuff."

UNDERSCORE

Note   Instead of the underscore, use *italics*, ALL CAPS, or SMALL CAPS to set off titles of books, magazines, movies, pamphlets, brochures, long poems, plays, or other literary works:

> I read *The New York Times* every Sunday.

> I read THE NEW YORK TIMES every Sunday.

Shadow Box	This is an example of an unshaded shadow box.

Shaded Shadow Box	This is an example of a shaded shadow box.

Assorted Rules

TYPING TIDBITS

Here are some tidbits:

Spacing As a general rule, space once after a punctuation mark, including the period at the end of a sentence.

Dash When you type a dash, use the special dash symbol (—), not two hyphens.

Emphasis Underscoring is passé. Use *italics*, **bold**, or SMALL CAPS.

Accent and Diacritical Marks Accent and diacritical marks are available with most software packages. If you are using Microsoft Word, go to the Insert menu, then Symbol. It is essential to use these marks to ensure accurate spelling of many foreign words, such as:

niño   Übermensch
à coup sûr   garçon

- To set off references to charts, pages, diagrams, etc.:

`The section on dinosaurs (pages 145–149) should`
`be...`

- To enclose numerals or letters that precede items in a series:

`I can be there on (1) Monday, June 1; (2) Tuesday,`
`June 2; or (3)...`

BRACKETS

- To include information added to something or someone being quoted:

`He said, "The length of the trial [from May 1`
`through June 15] caused..."`

- To enclose parenthetical information within parentheses:

`Your order (which included a dozen red pens [that`
`are not available] and five dozen blue pens) will`
`be...`

QUESTION MARKS

- At the end of a direct question:

`May we expect you by noon tomorrow?`

- After each question in a series of short questions that relate to the same subject and verb:

`Can you be there on Monday, June 1? Or on Tuesday,`
`June 2?`

- When a sentence begins as a statement and ends as a question:

`The store made the delivery on September 16, didn't`
`they?`

- To express uncertainty about a stated fact:

`On September 16 (?) the store made the delivery.`

Office aches, pain, and fatigue…Why suffer? A simple modification of your workspace and habits, and a little exercise done at your desk, can go a long way in preventing pain in the neck, shoulders, and back; headaches; eye strain; fatigue; carpal tunnel syndrome (CTS) or tendinitis; and a host of other pains and injuries associated with sedentary occupations.

Ergonomics

Ergonomics is a term that combines the Greek word *ergon*, meaning "work," and the English word *(eco)nomics*, which ultimately goes back to a Greek word that means "one who manages a household." Simply stated, it is "the study and management of the relationship between the worker and the environment." Ergonomics addresses the physical, physiological, and psychological requirements of each of us. In this section, we discuss the physical requirements.

Seating

Because you'll spend most of your time seated, one of the most important components is your chair. Look for a chair that has a sturdy base with four or five legs set on free-wheeling casters. It should also have armrests to help relieve the pressure on the wrist.

- Before expressions such as *for example*, *that is*, *namely*, etc.:

```
That's available in two colors; namely, blue and
green.
```

COLONS

- After a formal introduction that includes or implies *the following*:

```
We expect to open new offices in each of these
locations: New Bedford,...
```

- To introduce a long direct quotation:

```
Senator Longwinded said: "...
```

- After a statement that introduces an explanation or example:

```
My recommendation is: Don't delay.
```

DASHES

- To set off a parenthetical expression you want to emphasize:

```
The movie—in case you're interested—will be at
the...
```

- Before a word that sums up a preceding series:

```
Bob, Beth, Donna, and Jim—these are my friends from
photography class.
```

- To indicate a summarizing thought or an afterthought:

```
I know that wasn't an easy decision—even for you.
```

- Before the name of an author or word that follows a direct quote:

```
"You can turn painful situations around through
laughter. If you can find humor in something, you
can survive it."

                                    —Bill Cosby
```

PARENTHESES

- To set off a parenthetical expression you want to deemphasize:

```
The move (in case you're interested) will be at
the...
```

The seat pan and cushion should accommodate your hips and buttocks without being too snug. The pan should be adjustable to tilt slightly forward for writing and slightly backward for keyboarding. If the seat pan isn't adjustable, look for a wedge-shaped cushion that can be positioned one way for writing and another for keyboarding. Lumbar cushions are available in a variety of shapes and sizes for proper body alignment.

Look for a chair that can be raised and lowered to accommodate your height so that your feet rest comfortably on the floor. Your calves should be perpendicular to the floor and your knees slightly higher than your hips to avoid excessive curvature of the lower back. If your feet don't rest comfortably on the floor, a slanted footrest can help support them.

Make sure that all mechanical adjustments on your chair can be made while you are seated.

Note

Even the best-designed chair won't make up for bad posture. Bad posture is the root of many physical problems. Your spine consists of interconnected bones, known as vertebrae. They form three major curves in your neck, back, and lower back. If these curves become flattened or exaggerated due to poor posture, your spine will be out of whack and you can experience pain. So, sit upright and don't slouch. Your back should be straight to support the upper part of your body.

Work Surface

The work surface for the average person—whatever *average* really means—should be between 26 and 29 inches from the floor. You'll be most comfortable when the work surface is slightly above elbow height. This allows you to rest your arms on the surface without leaning too far forward. An adjustable shelf for the keyboard will help lessen the strain on your forearms and wrists.

Monitor

Headaches and eyestrain can result from being too close or too far from the monitor. The monitor should be between 18 and 28 inches away from you, and the top of the screen should be even with your forehead.

Keyboard

The proper height and position of the keyboard are essential to avoiding wrist problems, such as CTS and tendinitis. Your best defense is a natural, relaxed position. Your arms should hang comfortably at your sides so that your shoulders aren't hunched. And your forearms should be at 90-degree angles to your arms. You don't want to reach up or down to the keyboard. To take the weight off your shoulders and back, rest your forearms on the armrests of your chair. Keep your fingers curved and placed as close to the keys as possible.

- To set off abbreviations, titles, and degrees that follow a name:

  `Max Lorenz, CPA, will be our guest speaker.`

- To set off contrasting expressions:

  `I'll be on vacation in March, not April.`

- To divide a sentence that starts as a statement and ends as a question:

  `You'll call her, won't you?`

- To separate items in reference works:

  `The answer is in Volume II, Chapter 3, line 12.`

- To separate words that are used for emphasis:

  `You've told me that many, many times before.`

- To separate adjectives in a series if the word *and* has been omitted:

  `She is a very intelligent, thoughtful person.`

- To separate figures that aren't related:

  `In 1994, 250 employees were...`

- To clarify a sentence that would otherwise be confusing:

  `Only two weeks before, I had lunch with him.`

SEMICOLONS

- To separate independent clauses in a compound sentence when no conjunction is used:

  `Pete will arrive at ten; George will arrive at eight.`

- To separate independent clauses joined by a conjunction when two or more commas are used in the sentence:

  `I like green, blue, and red; but she likes...`

- Between coordinate clauses of a compound sentence that are joined by a parenthetical word or phrase:

  `We will meet again tomorrow; therefore, the project will continue.`

- To separate items in a series when the items themselves contain commas:

  `I can be there on Monday, June 1; Tuesday, June 2; or Thursday, June 4.`

There are devices on the market that are designed to protect against repetitive stress injuries. One of these devices is a wrist rest. Wrist rests may be purchased separately, or they may be built right into the keyboard, as below.

Lighting

Lighting experts have found that indirect, ceiling-mounted, or ambient lighting, in combination with a desk lamp, works best to eliminate problems associated with lighting. If you find that glare and brightness are a problem, purchase an antiglare screen.

Source Documents

Source documents—or this book—should be parallel with the monitor. The viewing distance should be between 24 and 36 inches. Keep your head erect and your eyes on the copy.

Exercises

If you sit for long periods of time, you'll force your muscles into a fixed position, causing fatigue and stiffness. Walking and stretching periodically can help relax the muscles. Try to get away from your desk for at least three minutes every hour. Additionally, simple exercises at your desk can help eliminate fatigue.

Breathing

With your eyes opened or closed, concentrate on breathing. Take five to ten long and deep breaths, inhaling through your nose and exhaling through your mouth.

Punctuation Potpourri

COMMAS

- Between items in an address or date:

  `On Monday, April 8, 19XX, he . . .`

- To set off an expression that explains the preceding word, name, or phrase:

  `Canal Avenue, our town's main street, will be . . .`

- Before a conjunction joining two independent clauses:

  `Pete will arrive at ten, and George will arrive at eight.`

- To set off words that directly address the person to whom you are speaking by name, title, or relationship:

  `Mr. Jones, please tell me . . .`

- After an introductory clause that is followed by what could be a complete sentence:

  `Unless you call, I will assume you will be here.`

- To set off an independent introductory expression that serves as an interjection:

  `Yes, I think so.`

- To set off an expression that if omitted would not change or destroy the meaning of the sentence:

  `My sister, who is wearing a brown suit, is a lawyer.`

- To surround a parenthetical word, phrase, or clause that interrupts the natural flow of the sentence:

  `We will, therefore, continue with the project.`

- To identify a person who is being directly quoted:

  `"I will be there tomorrow," she indicated.`

- To separate items in a series of three or more items:

  `Bob enjoys ice cream, candy, and potato chips.`

Eyes	At least once every hour look away from the monitor and focus on an object 15 to 20 feet away.
	A wonderful exercise for eye relaxation is to rub your hands together briskly until your palms feel warm. Make shallow cups and gently place your palms over your eyes. Without pressing on your eyes, make sure no light enters. Hold your palms over your eyes for at least 30 seconds. For a little variety while your eyes are covered, roll both eyes to the left and back to the middle. Do this five times, then do the same exercise rolling both eyes to the right.
Hands and Wrists	Every 15 to 30 minutes stretch your arms out to your side and over your head. Massage your hands and wrists to improve circulation. Don't forget to massage the spaces between your fingers and the areas around your nails. Flex your fingers and do wrist stretches frequently.
Neck	While breathing deeply, tilt your head toward your left shoulder, then toward your right shoulder. Then, with your head in a forward position, drop your chin to your chest and raise it slightly back.
	As a variation, keep your head upright. Look over your left shoulder several times, then over your right shoulder several times.
Back and Arms	Hold your right elbow with your left hand. Gently push the elbow toward your left shoulder. Hold the stretch for five seconds. Repeat this exercise with the left elbow.
	Interlace your fingers and lift your arms over your head, keeping your elbows straight. Press them as far back as you can without causing discomfort.
Note	All these exercises are intended for people who are in reasonably good health. If you experience any pain or discomfort while doing them, stop immediately and consult your doctor.

sans serif	A typeface without serifs.
	This is an example of sans serif type.
search engine	A software program that finds and retrieves information stored on the Internet. Popular search-engine providers include Google, MSN, and Yahoo!
serif	A fine line that finishes the main strokes of a character.
	This is an example of serif type.
software	The programs and routines needed to give a computer instructions.
spam	Unsolicited and unwanted junk mail delivered through email.
text message **or** *text*	A message typed on an alphanumeric keypad that is sent to or from a cell phone, hand-held computer, pager, or email address.
toggle	To shift, by means of a *toggle switch*, from one operation to another.
uppercase	Letters that are capitalized.
variable	Subject to change or something that is subject to change.
white space	A planned area of empty space, giving a document an open and airy look.
World Wide Web **or** *WWW* **or** *Web*	A system of interlinked hypertext documents accessed via the Internet.
WYSIWYG	[*What You See Is What You Get*] A system or program that displays on a screen exactly what you will see on the printed page.

PART TWO
Learning to Type

MODULE 1

Home Row Keys

home row keys

---

kilobyte (k or K)	1,024 bytes of information or storage space.
LAN	[*Local Area Network*] A system in which electronic equipment is connected to form a network within a limited area, such as a building or group of buildings.
landscape	Horizontal page orientation.
lowercase	Letters that are not capitalized.
memory	The capacity of a computer to store data and programs. *See also* RAM and ROM.
menu	A list of available options or commands displayed on a monitor.
modem	[*Modulator + Demodulator*] A device that converts data from one form into another, as from digital to analog and vice versa, so that it can be transmitted between a computer and a telephone.
monospacing	Spacing in which each character takes up the same amount of space.
off-line	Not connected to or dependent on a computer or computer network.
on-line	Connected to, dependent on, or accessible by means of a computer or computer network.
output	Data produced by a computer.
peripheral	A piece of equipment, such as a monitor, printer, or modem, that is added to a computer to give it additional functionality.
pixel	The smallest image-forming unit on a monitor.
point	A unit of measure used to specify type sizes.
program	A sequence of instructions for a computer.
proportional spacing	Spacing in which each character takes up a different amount of space, depending on its size. For example, the character *i* takes up less space than the character *w*.
RAM	[*Random-Access Memory*] Information the computer uses to run a program. RAM is temporary memory that is erased when the computer is turned off.
ROM	[*Read-Only Memory*] Information the computer uses to run the systems. ROM is permanent memory that is not erased when the computer is turned off.

DON'T TURN YOUR COMPUTER ON YET.

HOME ROW

The home row represents the keys on which you initially place your fingers. You will always return your fingers to the home row.

Left [A][S][D][F]   The keys for your left hand are [A] [S] [D] [F].

Right [J][K][L][;]   The keys for your right hand are [J] [K] [L] [;].

[Space Bar]   Before you start to type, familiarize yourself with two additional keys: [Space Bar] and
[Enter]   [Enter]. Find them on your computer.

Finger Positions   Place your fingers on the home row. Curve your fingers slightly and place them as close to the keys as possible.

Now, with a quick stroke, strike the [Space Bar] several times with your left thumb and then several times with your right thumb. Zip your right pinkie to the [Enter] key.

TURN YOUR COMPUTER ON.

Place your fingers on the appropriate keys on the home row and repeat the above exercise until the movement feels comfortable.

Remember:

- Strike [Enter] at the end of each line.
- Keep your eyes on the copy, not on your fingers.

Note   If you're using a font that is proportionally spaced, your letters won't line up at the right margin. That's OK.

Type   SAY EACH LETTER AS YOU STRIKE IT

email or *e-mail*	An Internet service that allows people to send and receive electronic messages, including files, audio, and video. Each email specifies the Internet address of each recipient.
e-zine	An electronic publication periodically delivered by email or posted on a website.
field	An area in a document for related information, such as names, addresses, or cities. For example:

NAME [   ]

font	An assortment of characters for one size and typeface. A font normally includes lightface and **boldface** and roman and *italic* characters and may often include small capitals.
format	The size, style, typeface, page size, margins, and printing requirements of a printed document.
hard copy	Computer-generated material that is printed on paper.
hardware	Computer equipment and peripherals.
HTML	[*Hypertext Markup Language*] HTML provides a language for formatting text and setting up links between documents. It is used extensively to design webpages.
http	[*Hypertext Transfer Protocol*] A procedure used to regulate the transfer of data, especially webpages, over the Internet.
input	Information that is entered into a system.
interface	The interaction, connection, or communication between two or more systems or devices.
instant messaging or *IMing*	Real-time communication between two or more computer or mobile device users facilitated by IM software. Popular software includes AIM (AOL Instant Messenger), Apple's iChat, Yahoo! Messenger, Skype Instant Messenger, MSN Chat, and more.
Internet	A system of interconnected private, public, academic, business, and government computer networks that exchange data around the world.
justification	The alignment of horizontal lines.

- left justify—text aligns at the left margin.
- right justify—text aligns at the right margin.
- center justify—text is centered.
- full justify—text aligns at left and right margins.

LEFT HAND ONLY

[A][S][D][F]

a aa aaa a aa aaa a aa aaa a aa aaa a aa aaa
a aa aaa a aa aaa a aa aaa a aa aaa a aa aaa

s ss sss s ss sss s ss sss s ss sss s ss sss
s ss sss s ss sss s ss sss s ss sss s ss sss

a aa aaa s ss sss a aa aaa s ss sss a aa aaa
s ss sss a aa aaa s ss sss a aa aaa s ss sss

d dd ddd d dd ddd d dd ddd d dd ddd d dd ddd
d dd ddd d dd ddd d dd ddd d dd ddd d dd ddd

f ff fff f ff fff f ff fff f ff fff f ff fff
f ff fff f ff fff f ff fff f ff fff f ff fff

d dd ddd f ff fff d dd ddd f ff fff d dd ddd
f ff fff d dd ddd f ff fff d dd ddd f ff fff

aa ss dd ff aa ss dd ff aa ss dd ff aa ss dd
aa ss dd ff aa ss dd ff aa ss dd ff aa ss dd

fff aaa sss ddd fff aaa sss ddd fff asdf adf
fff aaa sss ddd fff aaa sss ddd fff asdf adf

asdf asdf asdf asdf asdf asdf asdf asdf
asdf asdf asdf asdf asdf asdf asdf asdf

Words

a as add adds fad sad a ass add fad fads sad

Remember:

- Strike [Enter] at the end of each line.
- Keep your eyes on the copy, not on your fingers.

Glossary

alphanumeric	Consisting of both alphabetical and numeric characters.
ASCII	[*American Standard Code for Information Interchange*] A standard format for representing characters. A text file is in ASCII format.
bit	[*Binary Digit*] The smallest unit of information in a computer.
blog	A website of logs (web + log = blog) maintained by a person or company. Blogs display postings in chronological order and usually include links to comments, descriptions of events, or other material that can include graphics or video.
byte	A sequence of bits, usually shorter than a word. A byte generally represents eight bits.
character	A letter, number, symbol, space, or punctuation mark.
command	An instruction to the computer to perform a certain function.
cps or *CPS*	[*Characters per Second*] The speed at which characters are generated.
CPU	[*Central Processing Unit*] The brains of the computer.
crash	A sudden failure of a computer program or system.
cursor	The movable indicator on a computer screen. It is usually an arrow, static I, blinking rectangle, or dash that indicates the place where your next character will appear.
debug	To locate and remove errors from a computer program.
disk or *diskette*	A thin, flat circular plate coated with a magnetic substance. It is used for recording and storing data.
edit	To revise text.

RIGHT HAND ONLY

[J][K][L][;]

```
j jj jjj j jj jjj j jj jjj j jj jjj j jj jjj
j jj jjj j jj jjj j jj jjj j jj jjj j jj jjj

k kk kkk k kk kkk k kk kkk k kk kkk k kk kkk
k kk kkk k kk kkk k kk kkk k kk kkk k kk kkk

j jj jjj k kk kkk j jj jjj k kk kkk j jj jjj
k kk kkk j jj jjj k kk kkk j jj jjj k kk kkk

l ll lll l ll lll l ll lll l ll lll l ll lll
l ll lll l ll lll l ll lll l ll lll l ll lll

; ;; ;;; ; ;; ;;; ; ;; ;;; ; ;; ;;; ; ;; ;;;
; ;; ;;; ; ;; ;;; ; ;; ;;; ; ;; ;;; ; ;; ;;;

l ll lll ; ;; ;;; l ll lll ; ;; ;;; l ll lll
; ;; ;;; l ll lll ; ;; ;;; l ll lll ; ;; ;;;

jj kk ll ;; jj kk ll ;; jj kk ll ;; jj kk ll
;; jj kk ll ;; jj kk ll ;; jkl; jkl; jkl; kk
jkl; jkl; jkl; jkl; jkl; jkl; jkl; jk;l kl;k
```

BOTH HANDS

```
a j s k d l f; aa jj ss; kk dd ll ff ;; aa s
a j s k d l f; aa jj ss; kk dd ll ff ;; aa s

a j s k d l f ; aa jj ss kk dd ll ff ;; asjk
a j s k d l f ; aa jj ss kk dd ll ff ;; asjk

; f l d k s j a ;; ff ll dd kk ss jj aa ;; f
; f l d k s j a ;; ff ll dd kk ss jj aa ;; f
```

If you are thinking of using your computer to   10
start up a home-based business, here are some tips   20
to keep in mind: Set aside a separate room in your   30
home where you can work; make use of the telephone   40
directory instead of driving in the car; keep your   50
frequently used essentials handy; establish ground   60
rules to keep distractions to a minimum; keep reg-   70
ular hours; establish a routine; establish a back-   80
up system; use a single calendar; break the day up   90
into segments; keep good records; and do not forgo   100
vacations.   102

1   2   3   4   5   6   7   8   9   10

Also, know your market; seek out free public-   10
ity; go after quality clients; prepare a marketing   20
schedule; charge what you are worth; make the most   30
of your billable time; make networking a priority;   40
learn from your mistakes; recognize growing pains;   50
be nice to people; and learn financial management.   60

1   2   3   4   5   6   7   8   9   10

Words

a as add ask asks a as add; ask asks sad dad
dads fad fads lad lads; flask lass ask; asks
dad dads; salad salads sad dad dads lad lads
fad fads flask lad;; flask lass ask asks dad
dads; salad salads sad dad dads lad lads fad

LEFT HAND [G]

[F] → [G]

Zip [F] finger to [G]

g gg ggg f ff fff g gg ggg f ff fff g gg ggg
g gg ggg f ff fff g gg ggg f ff fff g gg ggg

a ss ddd f gg aaa s dd fff g aa sss d ff ggg
a ss ddd f gg aaa s dd fff g aa sss d ff ggg

RIGHT HAND [H]

[J] ← [H]

Zip [J] finger to [H]

j jj jjj h hh hhh j jj jjj h hh hhh j jj jjj
j jj jjj h hh hhh j jj jjj h hh hhh j jj jjj

j kk lll ; hh jjj k ll ;;; h jj kkk l ;; hhh
j jj jjj h hh hhh j jj jjj h hh hhh j jj jjj

Words

all fall falls hall halls; glad ash dash ask
as ask gash hash; glass flask lash; slash as
lads glass sash all fall falls hall; halls;;
glad ash dash gash hash glass flask lash all
slash lads glass sash;; fall shall; gash lag

fall hall gash dash lash sash lads; shall had
ash flash; ask flask dash all fall hall; lash
hash dash; asks; flasks halls; falls; has jag
ash flash; ask flask dash all fall hall; lash
all hall gash dash lash sash lads; shall jags

Often, the terms keyboarding and typewriting   10
are used interchangeably. Both are operations that   20
involve data being entered on a keyboard. There is   30
a slight difference. When you are typewriting on a   40
typewriter, your input appears right on the paper.   50
When you are keyboarding on a computer, your input   60
appears on the screen. You have the opportunity to   70
edit and make any changes without ever using those   80
old-fashioned pencil erasers or carbon paper. When   90
you are ready to print a paper copy, you only need   100
to give the computer the command. In a few moments   110
you will have a paper copy of the data you expect.   120

1   2   3   4   5   6   7   8   9   10
_____

The world is full of color. Color adds much impact   10
to anything we see and do. Color can create a mood   20
or help in separating the ripe from the unripe. It   30
has impact on us in a number of ways. For example,   40
red can invoke feelings of danger or excitement or   50
tell us to stop. White is used to represent clean,   60
pure, and honest feelings. Black is used to invoke   70
feelings of heaviness, death, or seriousness. Pink   80
shouts of youth, femininity, and warmth. And green   90
indicates growth, comfort, positiveness, and tells   100
us to go. Color has a lot of meaning to all of us.   110
It's being used in many psychological experiments.   120

1   2   3   4   5   6   7   8   9   10
_____

BRAIN BUSTER #2   *28-Letter Word*

What's a 28-letter word that means "a doctrine against the dissolution of the establishment"?

_ _

The answer is on page 193.

You can use abbreviations for many purposes. There   10
is one basic rule, however: "If in doubt, write it   20
out." Generally, abbreviate academic degrees, such   30
as B.A., M.A., Ph.D., or professional titles, such   40
as R.N., Esq., Rev. Abbreviate the common names of   50
companies, organizations, and government agencies,   60
such as AT&T, MCI, IBM, YMCA, YWCA, FAA, HEW, EPA.   70
Acronyms are formed from letters in long titles or   80
phrases. Some familiar acronyms are OPEC, NOW, and   90
DOS. Do keep in mind: "If in doubt, write it out."   100

1   2   3   4   5   6   7   8   9   10
_____

Telecommunications is a link between the worlds of   10
word processing and data processing and the audio-   20
visual industry. Telecommunications transmits both   30
oral and written communication from one machine to   40
another in a different location. Cables interfaced   50
with computers allow you to patronize your depart-   60
ment store, query your local library, or ascertain   70
information on your bank accounts. Now, conference   80
calls are used to allow people in remote locations   90
to conduct business meetings without being face to   100
face. Telecommunications curtails time and travel!   110

1   2   3   4   5   6   7   8   9   10
_____

Top Row Keys

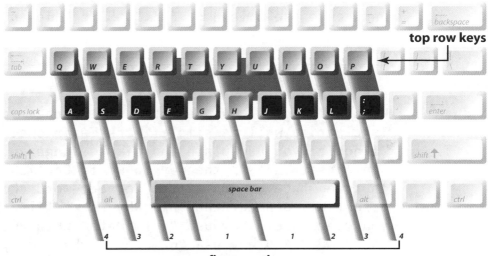

top row keys

finger paths

Note: Keys are spaced apart to depict finger paths.

You will be moving your fingers off the home row, but they should always return to the original keys on the home row.

[T]   Zip [F] finger to [T]

[T]
↗
[F]

f ff fff t tt ttt f ff fff t tt ttt f ff fff
f ff fff t tt ttt f ff fff t tt ttt f ff fff

fftt ftft fftt ftft ff tt ftt fff tt f r trt
fftt ftft fftt ftft ff tt ftt fff tt f r trt

Words   that lath task tall tads dash had tall hall;
fat; flask flat fast; sash tads lads; sat as
halls halts fast asks; dash that shalt shall
fast last all; gash stall lath had tall; all

Jo was given $534,789 on April 4, 1994, and $3,567   10
on June 16, 1994. This resulted in total assets of   20
$538,356. "What'll you do with so much money?" her   30
sister asked. "Oh, I guess I'll invest some in the   40
stock market, deposit some in my bank, and buy new   50
furniture with the rest." "Uh, can I ask a favor?"   60
Jo's sister Catherine asked hesitantly. "I'm broke   70
and could use a loan of $75." "Sure," Jo answered.   80

1   2   3   4   5   6   7   8   9   10

USE CLEAR AND SIMPLE LANGUAGE   6
When writing, always be sure the language you pick   16
is clear as well as simple. Mark Twain once wrote,   26
"I notice you use plain and simple language, brief   36
sentences. That is the way to write English." That   46
is true whatever you write. Correct word choice is   56
essential to understanding. Why use "utilize" when   66
you mean "use"? Why use "terminate" when you could   76
use "end"? And why use "numerous" when "many" will   86
say it clearly? That IS the way to write English!!   96

1   2   3   4   5   6   7   8   9   10

        The following words are commonly misspelled.   10
How many of them can you type correctly? eligible,   20
appropriate, embarrass, oblige, paid, maintenance,   30
truly, similar, separate, exhaust, minimum, a lot,   40
questionnaire, reference, perseverance, Wednesday,   50
endorsement, knowledge, unanimous, until, foreign,   60
February, forty, unnecessary, sympathy, interpret,   70
extraordinary, feasible, library, dissatisfactory,   80
disbursement, bookkeeping, beneficial, convenient,   90
abbreviation, cannot, bankrupt, its, and surprise.   100

1   2   3   4   5   6   7   8   9   10

[R]
[R]

↖

   [F]

Zip [F] finger to [R]

```
f ff fff r rr rrr f ff fff r rr rrr f ff fff
f ff fff r rr rrr f ff fff r rr rrr f ff fff

fftt fftt ffrr ffrr ff tt ftt frr tt trtf fr
ttrr ftft fftr ftrr ff rr ftt fff rt rtfr tf
```

Words

```
hath lath shalt fall rash fast last lash ask
fall falls; asks tall trash grass sash; hats
flask hall halt gash grass lass rash ash; as
rash shalt fall fast; last ask rats rash rag
```

[E]
[E]

↖

   [D]

Zip [D] finger to [E]

```
d dd ddd e ee eee d dd ddd e ee eee d dd ddd
d dd ddd e ee eee d dd ddd e ee eee d dd ddd

ddee ddee deed eede eded edft edrt reft deft
eede ddde ertf gfrt getd ttfr tred grdt fret
```

Words

```
ate rag had fat eel eels feel heel slat gall
had sat had fat eels eel heel feel gall slat
tree fled sled held tasks last ask sale tall

glad fled sled held; task last ask sale tall
data date late; talk lath let fatal atlas as
sealed false feeds faded; tested raffle eggs
```

[U]
[U]

↖

   [J]

Zip [J] finger to [U]

```
j jj jjj u uu uuu j jj jjj u uu uuu j jj j
j jj jjj u uu uuu j jj jjj u uu uuu u uu u

ju jjuu jjuujjuu ju jjuu jjuuj juu uju
ju jjuu jjuujjuu ju jjuu jjuuj juu uju

jjuu jjuu juju juju uujj ujuj jjuu juju juj
jjuu jjuu juju juju uujj ujuj jjuu juju juj
```

Although spelling checkers are wonderful, they are 10
not able to distinguish between homonyms (or words 20
that sound alike) and commonly confused words. For 30
example, you would use "principle" to mean "value" 40
or "rule"; you should use the spelling "principal" 50
when you mean that something is "main" or "chief." 60

| 1 | 2 | 3 | 4 | 5 | 6 | 7 | 8 | 9 | 10 |

Commas are used to set off the individual elements 10
of an address except for Zip Codes. As an example, 20
you would write Mr. and Mrs. Arthur Bainless, 2305 30
Main Street, Monsey, NY 10952. If a preposition is 40
used between the elements, you would not place the 50
comma between the elements. As an example, Mr. Jon 60
Doe of One Madison Avenue in Washington, DC 20233. 70

| 1 | 2 | 3 | 4 | 5 | 6 | 7 | 8 | 9 | 10 |

What is the most efficient means of communication? 10
If you said the computer, there are many who might 20
disagree. For example, for half a millennium books 30
were the most efficient form of written communica- 40
tions. And then there is the long-neglected art of 50
face-to-face communication, which has made way for 60
earphones, CDs, camcorders. So much for high tech! 70

| 1 | 2 | 3 | 4 | 5 | 6 | 7 | 8 | 9 | 10 |

Words	us lug hug dug sue due just adjust rust after rested stalk feud feuds feudal fuel fuels has after as used useful duffle fuss fuse refuses

refused suede auks ukulele restful true user
just adjust; rust gust; hurt hurl; furl dash
shut huts ruts glut ruffle raffle hassle use

[I]	Zip [K] finger to [I]
[I]	
↖	
[K]	

j jj jj i ii ii j jj jj i ii ii ji ji ji
j jj jj i ii ii j jj jj i ii ii ji ji ji

jjii jjii iijj jiji jiji ijij jiii jjjij
jii jjii iijj jiji jiji ijij jiii jjjiji

Words	just sits west feast least listed used its listless tilted asked whisk; whisked; wish wished washer aid laid said lust list last

waist rut aide aides rust rested listed it
rest; fist fish; gist this that risk; kite
skies skit huts rested tried fried hied it

Let's Shift

[Shift]	There is a [Shift] key on each side of your keyboard. [Shift] keys are used to capitalize letters or type the symbols or characters on the top of the keys on which more than one character is shown.
[Caps Lock]	Locate the [Caps Lock] key on your keyboard. This is used when you want to capitalize a series of letters and do not want to hold down the [Shift].
Left [Shift]	Press the left [Shift] quickly and firmly with your left pinkie while simultaneously pressing any letter with your right hand.
Right [Shift]	Press the right [Shift] in the same manner with your right pinkie and simultaneously press any letter with your left hand.

Lindsell & Sons (our big competitor) was selected.   10
"Successful Investments" was in the paper in July.   20
Her mother's a 75-year-old retired French teacher.   30
The enrollment of 350 is only half of that needed.   40

1   2   3   4   5   6   7   8   9   10

On September 21, 562 people attended the seminars.   10
I saw Mr. Goldberg on May 22, June 13, and July 5.   20
Almost 16,789,645 new people registered last year.   30
October 5 marks the 25th anniversary of the store.   40
Sally quit her job and applied for a new one here.   50

1   2   3   4   5   6   7   8   9   10

On December 15, 1992, we sent them a check for $7.   10
In 1987, six members were eligible for promotions.   20
At least 25% of the stock must be sold by April 3.   30
Check No. 21 was issued by the company last March.   40
Because he was tired, Elliot played only one game.   50

1   2   3   4   5   6   7   8   9   10

If he's elected president of the class, there will   10
be lots of changes. He's even planning a number of   20
side trips. One will be to New York City; one will   30
be to Washington, DC; one will be to Phillipsburg,   40
New Jersey; and the rest haven't been decided yet.   50

1   2   3   4   5   6   7   8   9   10

The chairman announced that seven people will have   10
to be laid off. That will create a big problem for   20
those involved because the names will be announced   30
just two days before the Christmas holiday. That's   40
a difficult time of year to initiate a job search.   50

1   2   3   4   5   6   7   8   9   10

Practice	H J K L ; U I hH jJ kK lL ;: uU iI Hj Kl ;:; L K J H ; lL kK jK hH I U :; lK jH iK uU :;: A S D F G E R T aA sS dD fF gG wW eE rR tT A A S D F G E R T aA sS dD fF gG wW eE rR tT A
Words	Lisa Dirk; Fall Sail; Were;; Worth Fort Sale; Shall Lads Flask Risk True ;; Jail Slid Slide Usury Lisa Tried To Sell; Last Her House Tied Sheila Field Fried Frieda Sits Hits Fists Ask Like Sake Glide Afraid Grade Irate Lasted; As Gust Adjusted Hustler Just Jester Kiss; Faker
[Caps Lock]	Press [Caps Lock]. Type the following exercise without pressing [Shift]. LISA DIRK CALL SAIL WERE WORTH FORT SALE TO SHALL LADS FLASK TRUE JAIL SLIDE USURY SLID TRIED LISTED; WAIST ATLAS FATAL SHALL; SLAT Press [Caps Lock] again to release.
[Q] *[Q]* ↖ *[A]*	Zip [A] finger to [Q] a aa aaa q qq qqq a aa aaa q qq qqq a aa aaa a aa aaa q qq qqq a aa aaa q qq qqq a aa aaa q qq qqq a aa aaa q qq qqqaq aaqq aaq qaa qqa q qq qqq a aa aaa q qq qqqaq aaqq aaq qaa qqa aqua qua aaqq qquu ququ aqua qaqa; aq aaqq qu aqua qua aaqq qquu ququ aqua qaqa; aq aaqq qu

Timed Typings

On Friday we should have an appointment for Arnie.   10
Josephine bought a new piano and sold the old one.   20
Janet bet fifteen dollars that her team would win.   30

1   2   3   4   5   6   7   8   9   10

T.J. Davis, the guest speaker, is a famous writer.   10
On my way here, I stopped to visit Sally and June.   20
Gracie returned the prize money she won yesterday.   30

1   2   3   4   5   6   7   8   9   10

Paul jumped when he saw the dog and cat run there.   10
Pauline Kelly worked hard to pass the examination.   20
Valerie greatly impressed the boys with her story.   30
Kyle fixed the broken chairs for Nancy and Sheila.   40

1   2   3   4   5   6   7   8   9   10

As Barbara requested, Norm will pay all the bills.   10
Jumping over the fence, she fell in the leaf pile.   20
Priscilla mixed her drink with fresh strawberries.   30
Donna was glad her family took a long summer trip.   40

1   2   3   4   5   6   7   8   9   10

Jon had a wonderful time at the party. However, he   10
had to leave early because he had to bring the car   20
to the garage before 1:00 that evening. If not, he   30
would have had to pay an additional $9 in charges.   40

1   2   3   4   5   6   7   8   9   10

Words

quit quite quiet quietest last lasted:; quest
Keith Year Kirk Dirk Ukuleles: equal; equaled
rust Quit IQ: quit quite; quiet quite quitter

quit quite sight quest request sequester aqua
just quail quake equate Hearsay hither quests
little Quail Isle Aisle thirst first rest ask

[O]
[O]
↖
　[L]

Zip [L] finger to [O]

l ll lll o oo ooo l ll lll o oo ooo lloo lolo
l ll lll o oo ooo l ll lll o oo ooo lloo lolo

lloo lloo ooll lolo olol lllo oool lllo oool;
lloo lloo ooll lolo olol lllo oool lllo oool;

Words

loot foot food hoot route Quote quo quiet too
should fool fold Kirk look looker risk; stool
fatal goat Route Four foe Quaff just Reject::

Other oath retell tread truth Aqua saddle Ooh
lather leather other oast joust quest Request
guest lust last list lost resist sadist Ho Ho

[W]
[W]
↖
　[S]

Zip [S] finger to [W]

s ss sss w ww www s ss sss w ww www ss ww sws
s ss sss w ww www s ss sss w ww www ss ww sws

ss ww sws ssww ssww wwss swsw wsws ss ww swsw
ss ww sws ssww ssww wwss swsw wsws ss ww swsw

Words

West wrist risk Quest; was wash washer washed
aqua tight write wrote queer quote quoter; we
Usual; Western Westerner waste stew: watered;

hid Stewart; stroke wrath wire rewire; where;
weird weirdo thought through throughout: what
whither; who whose row resod Walt Walter Welt

PROGRESS CHART

Date	Total WPM	Errors	Adjusted WPM	Date	Total WPM	Errors	Adjusted WPM	Date	Total WPM	Errors	Adjusted WPM

[P]

Zip [;] finger to [P]

↖

     [;]

```
; ;; ;;; p pp ppp ; ;; ;;; p pp ppp ;;p pp; ;
; ;; ;;; p pp ppp ; ;; ;;; p pp ppp ;;p pp; ;

pp;; pp; ;p; pp; ;;p pp;; ;p p; ;;pp pp; ;;pp
pp;; pp; ;p; pp; ;;p pp;; ;p p; ;;pp pp; ;;pp
```

Words

```
Puppy equip; perk; park pot post pots; repot;
potter potted deport depart parted pester; pa
upper; Upper; dapper; flapper preppy; parade;

equip; Equipped: put puts putter putt; poise;
hope; hoped quake; parka; Parker; Pastor Will
Wipple Flower Power How; Pill Poll Pull: poet
```

[Y]
[Y][U]

Zip [J] finger to [Y]

↖

     [J]

```
j jj jj y yy yy j jj jj y yy yy jj yy jj yy j
j jj jj y yy yy j jj jj y yy yy jj yy jj yy j

juy yuj jjuuyy yyuujj ju jy yuj juy jjyy juyj
juy yuj jjuuyy yyuujj ju jy yuj juy jjyy juyj
```

Words

```
You Your Yours; Youth Petty pretty poise; yet
yet; yesterday doily putty yuppie puppy; puts
putter putty silky yellow shalt hold Yodel Ye

Hear Ye; willowy salty peppery; quilt purse::
Aye; Yes; guess Westerly: Easterly: Southerly
Disk dusk Trust topper trip warp; wrap; kites
```

Words per Minute (wpm)

Take a look at the example above. Notice that five characters—letters, spaces, and punctuation marks—count as one word. Each line on the above scale has seven words.

1. If you type the first line in one minute, you would type 7 wpm. If you type both lines in one minute, you would type 14 wpm.
2. If you complete a partial line, select the number on the scale nearest to the point at which you stopped. For example, assume you set the timer for one minute and type the following:

```
Pat adjusted the rig where it tore.
Dad adjust
```

Add the first line completed	7
to the part of the second line completed.	+2
Total	9 wpm

3. To get the adjusted wpm, deduct from your total the number of words you misspelled. (Count only one error even if the word has several incorrect letters.) That will give you the total number of correctly typed wpm.
4. If you took a timing that was for more than one minute, divide the number of minutes into your total. For example, assume you typed 60 words in 3 minutes.

$$60 \div 3 = 20 \text{ wpm}$$

Timing Tips

Taking a Timed Typing

1. When you are ready to begin, set a timer for 1–5 minutes, depending on your level of skill.

Hints

- When you are in the early learning stages, limit your timings to one minute each.
- When you can type approximately 30 wpm, increase your timings to two and three minutes.
- Longer timings will help you develop the ability to type for longer periods of time.

2. Try to block out all surrounding noise.
3. Remember to keep your eyes on the copy, not on the keyboard. If you think you hit the wrong key, do not look up to verify it. Just continue typing.
4. Type until the timer rings. If you finish the timing and the timer has not rung, start that timing again.
5. Practice typing the words you misspelled.

It is time to check your progress. Please refer to Appendix A, beginning on page 174, to learn how to take a timed typing and figure out your words per minute (wpm).

```
stop adjusted the hip where it rest          7
quit feasted that was there it oust         14
haul there today was after you left         21
saw a Iris dog to the old Paul door         28
she left Quaker: us in lasts yearly         35

1       2       3       4       5       6       7
```

7 wpm = fair
14 wpm = good
21 wpm = very good
28 wpm = excellent
35 wpm = superior

BRAIN BUSTER #3   *Three Consecutive Double Letters*

Name a word in the English language that has three consecutive double letters.

A possible answer is on page 193.

Appendixes

APPENDIX A

*How to Take a Timed Typing
and Figure Your Speed*

Practice, Practice, Practice!

Before you take a timed typing, it is important to practice. Select a timing to practice. This is a wonderful way to build your speed and learn how many words per minute (wpm) you type.

First, focus on accuracy. Type the timing for one minute as fast as you can without making any errors. Circle each error you made. If you made more than two errors in the one-minute period, slow down slightly and try again. Repeat the exercise until you can type the timing with no errors.

Second, focus on speed. Type the timing as fast as you can without worrying about errors. Then, type the same timing again, pushing for a few more words per minute. Repeat this exercise until you feel you cannot type one additional word and still have your text recognizable.

Third, take the timing. Your goal is to type the timing as fast as you can without making any errors.

Calculating Your Words Per Minute

Example of Timed Typing

```
Pat adjusted the rig where it tore.        7
Dad adjusted the hat where it tore.       14

 1    2    3    4    5    6    7
```

Bottom Row Keys

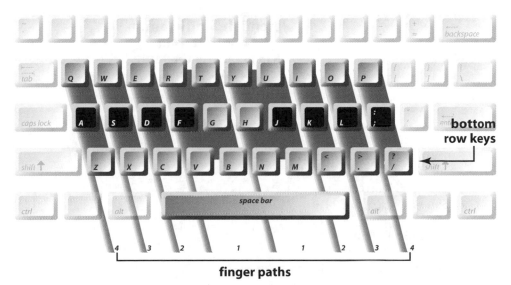

finger paths

Note: Keys are spaced apart to depict finger paths.

You will be moving your fingers off the home row, but they should always return to the home row.

Let's Review

Home Row

```
aa ss dd ff aa ss dd ff aa ss dd ff aa ss dd
aa ss dd ff aa ss dd ff aa ss dd ff aa ss dd

fff aaa sss ddd fff aaa sss ddd fff asdf adf
fff aaa sss ddd fff aaa sss ddd fff asdf adf

asdf asdf asdf asdf asdf asdf asdf asdf
asdf asdf asdf asdf asdf asdf asdf asdf
```

Sample Cover Letter for Someone Graduating

Type the following cover letter exactly as you see it.

Jeremiah Smithsonian
14 Seahawk Trail
San Francisco, CA 94107
(415) 362-1994

March 2, 20—

Ms. Arnelle Perkins
Human Resources Manager
Associated Laboratories, Inc.
405 Morris Street
San Francisco, CA 94107

Dear Ms. Perkins:

Subject: Position as Research Assistant

I am responding to your ad for a research assistant which appeared in *The Boston Globe*. I believe that I have the qualifications you're looking for.

While I was in college, I held many internships, as you can see from my resume. These positions gave me insights into the business world, into working in laboratories, and into working with other professionals. I would like to use the skills I have acquired to build my career at Associated Laboratories.

Next step
I'll call you next week to set up an interview. Thank you.

Sincerely yours,

Jeremiah Smithsonian

```
l ll lll ; ;; ;;; l ll lll ; ;; ;;; l ll lll
; ;; ;;; l ll lll ; ;; ;;; l ll lll ; ;; ;;;

jj kk ll ;; jj kk ll ;; jj kk ll ;; jj kk ll
;; jj kk ll ;; jj kk ll ;; jkl; jkl; jkl; kk
jkl; jkl; jkl; jkl; jkl; jkl; jkl; jk;l kl;k
```

If you have difficulty with any words or specific letters, practice them.

Home Row Words
```
all fall falls hall halls; glad Ash dash ask
lads glass Sash ALL fall falls hall; halls;;
glad ash dash gash hash glass Flask lash all
slash lads glass sash;; fall shall; gash lag
```

Home Row and
Top Row Words
```
that LATH task tall tads dash had tall hall;
fat; flask flat fast; sash tads lads; sat as
flask hall halt hath GRASS lass rash ash; as
rash shalt fall fast; Last ASK sash rash rag

data date late talk lath let fatal atlas ass
sealed false feeds faded; tested raffle eggs
refused Suede auks ukulele restful true user
rest use fist Fish; gist this that risk kite

skies skit; huts rested tried:: fried hied it
rust Quit IQ: quit quite: quiet quite quitter
loot foot food hoot route Quote quo quiet too
should fool fold Kirk look looker risk; stool

whither; who whose row resod Walt Walter Welt
Wipple Flower Power How; Pill Poll Pull: poet
You Your Yours; Youth Petty pretty poise; yet
yet; yesterday doily puppy yuppie putty; puts
```

Sample Cover Letter for Someone in the Workforce

Type the following cover letter exactly as you see it.

Jason Randall
10 James Road, Ipswich, MA 01938
978-356-2231
Jason_Randall@hotmail.com

September 12, 20—

Mr. James Coogan
Human Resources Director
AL&M Insurance
334 Topsfield Road
Sterling, MA 01564

Dear Mr. Coogan:

Subject: Position of Business Systems Analyst

Jon Smith, your IT Manager, mentioned that you have an immediate opening for a business systems analyst. Jon and I worked together at Barrington Chemical Company for more than ten years. He can attest to my qualifications and strong work ethics.

I am experienced in system development, implementation, and production support, and have extensive experience with writing conversion specifications, developing and executing user test plans, and data quality analysis. I am also skilled in Oracle SQL, TOAD, TOra, Crystal Reports, COGNOS, and MedStat.

Next step
I will call you next week to set up a mutually convenient time for us to meet. Thank you.

Sincerely,

Jason Randall

[C]
[D]
  ↘
    [C]

Zip [D] finger to [C]

d dd ddd e ee eee d dd ddd c cc ce dd ccdd
d dd ddd e ee eee d dd ddd c cc ce dd ccdd

ddcc drdc ccdd dec eecc ddcc decd ddce dc
ddcc drdc ccdd dec eecc ddcc decd ddce dc

ccdd ccddee ccddee eeddcc edc cde dec cde
ccdd ccddee ccddee eeddcc edc cde dec cde

Words

scarf call cold collar called chattel ace
scold Charles Charlie Carol Carole; Scots
scrap Pacific; specific special creed PAC

Scout race races racer raced trace traced
Crow crawls fiercest Copper Scary; DC Car
Cold Colder Coldest;; recall acquire; icy

[V]
[F]
  ↘
    [V]

Zip [F] finger to [V]

f ff ff r rr rr f ff ff c cc cc ff cc frc
f ff ff r rr rr f ff ff c cc cc ff cc frc

f ff ff c cc cc v vv vv f ff ff ff cc vv
f ff ff c cc cc v vv vv f ff ff ff cc vv

ffcc ffvv ccvv fcvf ffrr ffcc ffvv frcvf
ffcc ffvv ccvv fcvf ffrr ffcc ffvv frcvf

fff ccc vvv rrr fff ccc vvv rrr fff vvvf
fff ccc vvv rrr fff ccc vvv rrr fff vvvf

EXERCISE 2

Sample Resume for Someone Graduating

Type the following one-page resume exactly as you see it.

MARCIA LINDSEY
14 Lorenz Lane
Spring Valley, New York 10977
(914) 362-1994

Education   Baldridge College, 1700 Union Blvd., Bayshore, NY
Degree: MS in Clinical Engineering
Graduation: March 2000

Baldridge College, Avenue J, Brooklyn, NY
Degree: BS Computer Science and Biology
Graduation: June 1997

Wellrock Community College, College Rd., Suffern, NY
Degree: AA in Liberal Arts
Graduation: 1994
Honors: Dean's List, Phi Sigma Omicron

Relevant Courses   Physiology for Engineers I and II, Genetics, Bioprocessing Laboratory,
Multivariate Analysis, Introduction to Research Methods, Microbiology,
Biomedical Instrumentation, Medical Device Safety and Design, Mechanical
Materials, Biomedical Engineering Laboratory, Electrophysiology Signal
Processing, Business/Management Skills in Biomedicine

Professional Experience   Nyack Hospital, Nyack, NY (10/99 - 1/00)
Position: Biomedical Intern
Responsibilities: Preventive Maintenance, Maintenance of Hospital Medical
Equipment

North Star Research, Bayshore, NY (3/99 - 6/99)
Position: Research Assistant
Environment: R & D, Bioengineering
Responsibilities: Research, Quality Control, Laboratory Maintenance

Neuromedical Systems, Inc., Suffern, NY (12/96 - 9/97)
Position: Customer Services Representative
Environment: Client/Server
Responsibilities: Customer Service, Database Maintenance, Software
Troubleshooting, Training New Customer Service Representatives

Computer Skills   SQL and Assembly Programming

---

vowel cover Voice Voiced Voiceless; veto
void avoid evade Cavern; Caverns Vacates
escape Very truly, Very truly yours, VIP

evasive evacuate evaporate Everett Evert
Value avocet avocado:: aversive; average
avid overall overly overt overtly; ovens

[B]
[F]
  ↘
[V][B]

Zip [F] finger to [B]

f ff ff r rr rr f ff ff c cc cc ff cc fc
f ff ff r rr rr f ff ff c cc cc ff cc fc

ffcc ffvv ccvv fcvf ffrr ffcc ffvv frcvf
ffcc ffvv ccvv fcvf ffrr ffcc ffvv frcvf

f ff fff v vv vvv b bb bbb fff bbb fcvbf
f ff fff v vv vvv b bb bbb fff bbb fcvbf

ff gg cc vv bb fgc vbf fgc cvb frcvb gbf
ff gg cc vv bb fgc vbf fgc cvb frcvb gbf

ccvvbb ffgg bb ffvvbb fgcvb fgcvb frgb f
ccvvbb ffgg bb ffvvbb fgcvb fgcvb frgb f

Words

about Bob Bobby Babble Cobbler Cable Boy
Ebb Tide: obviate obvious obtuse oboe oh
Ibis brash breach brush Brutal; brutish;

Babbitt babassu BB babushka bacillus Bad
bachelor baby blue eyes: backyard backed
backlog abrasive abvolt abyss obscured:;

SpeakEasy, Inc., Nashua, NH 1996–1997

Three-year-old start-up specializing in speech recognition software, purchased by VCS in 1997, later purchased by Philips N.V.

Director of Engineering
- Directed all engineering efforts for rev 2.0 release of Automatic Speech Recognition Software and succeeded in shipping product on time.
- Developed customer documentation, training and managed the beta program.
- Established product teams, managed product plans and schedules. Working closely with marketing, obtained customer feedback, identified new product features.

Principal Engineer for port to NT 4.0
- Led the engineering effort to port ASR Software from SCO Unix to Windows/NT, forcing a major redesign of the internal architecture to support Win32 threads and DLL modules.
- Defined and developed network-based regression and stress test system for ASR software. System simulated more than 20 simultaneous phone calls and measured major aspects of system performance with a repeatability within 2%.

DataComm Corporation, Greenfield, MA 1980–1996

Fortune 500 mini-computer manufacturer with world-wide operations

Software Staff Specialist, Network Systems Engineering Division, 1992–1996
- Conceptualized, obtained corporate commitment for, designed, implemented and shipped an ONC/RPC and SNMP-based agent to manage a proprietary disk array (Roncal) on Unix and Windows/NT systems. Evolved into EMC's Navisphere product.
- Developed extensions to ONC/RPC to provide asynchronous operation for a Unix clustering product.
- Provided significant amount of custom engineering for major federal opportunity for network management.

Education

M.S. in Engineering, University of California, Berkeley (3.8 GPA)

[M]
[J]
  ↘
    [M]

Zip [J] finger to [M]

```
j jj jjj m mm mm j jj jjj m mm mmm jmjm
j jj jjj m mm mm j jj jjj m mm mmm jmjm

jj mm jmjm jmjm mm jj jj hh mm jhm jhmj
jj mm jmjm jmjm mm jj jj hh mm jhm jhmj

jj uu jj hh jj mm juj jhj jmj juhm jumj
jj uu jj hh jj mm juj jhj jmj juhm jumj

jjmm mmjj mmhh jjuu uumm uujmm mmjuu jm
jjmm mmjj mmhh jjuu uumm uujmm mmjuu jm
```

Words

jump jumble jumbled Jack Jackass eject;
Jam James Jamie Jameson Jackson; Jesse:
object objects objected ambulate ambled

embryo obsess obsolesce oblate Obie Moe
Moth Mothy Mother Mister Miss moist Met
William Math Mathematics move moved mop

[X]
[S]
  ↘
    [X]

Zip [S] finger to [X]

```
s ss ss x xx xx ss xx ss xx sx sx sssxx
s ss ss x xx xx ss xx ss xx sx sx sssxx

ssww ssxx swx swx xxx sss www swx sxw x
ssww ssxx swx swx xxx sss www swx sxw x

ssxx ssww swxs swxs ssxw swxs ssxw swxs
ssxx ssww swxs swxs ssxw swxs ssxw swxs

sswwxx sssxxx ssswxx ssxwwx ssxw wsxswx
sswwxx sssxxx ssswxx ssxwwx ssxw wsxswx
```

Allen Roberts
aroberts@aol.com

508-666-3334
5 Westminster Road, Marlborough, MA 01752

Professional Highlights

Accomplished software engineer with extensive experience in Linux, Windows NT, Device Drivers, and Enterprise-class storage systems. Five years' experience in product marketing with a comprehensive understanding of the business issues of software development from vision to market launch. Proven track record working in both small and large development environments.

- Created and developed a new product to manage DataComm's Roncal storage sub-system that was later adopted by Roncal and has evolved into AMC's Novapro product.
- Managed a small group of young developers at SpeakEasy that resulted in the development of three new speech recognition applications and a new version of the speech recognition engine. All four projects were completed on time.
- At Quartell, with a very small development group, created and developed a new thin-server appliance. Accomplished this in less than six months, from concept to fully functional (hardware and software).

Technical Expertise

- *Languages:* C/C++, AWK, bash, make, CVS, RCS, postscript, groff, lex, yacc
- *Operating Systems:* Redhat Linux 6.0 - 7.3, WINDOWS/NT, WIN32 API, Unix (V.4.2), MS-DOS
- *Interfaces:* i2c, SCSI, ATA, SCSI tape and media changer, SNMP, ONC/RPC

Professional Experience

Quartell | ATZ, Worcester, MA, 1997–present

Staff Engineer – Reporting to Quartell / ATZ CTO
Designed, procured and managed a new development lab. Responsible for the lab, office systems and local area network for 30 systems and 8 engineers.

Lead Engineer for DX30, an embedded Linux virtual tape library, launched fall of 2002
- Codeveloped a working proof-of-concept of the virtual library with multiple tape drives and changer. Demonstrated to Quartell CEO and executive staff resulting in corporate commitment and funding for the project.
- Developed Linux device drivers including Q Fibre Channel running in SCSI target mode, Hant24x4 LCD display, system monitoring of temperature, fans, and voltages using LM87 and LM75, and a high performance buffer manager between the Fibre channel and Linux I/O subsystem. Enhanced standard Linux USB 2.0 and RAID5 drivers.

Xe sexy xylan xyster xiphoid; xebec; ax
six sex Xmas sixty Exit Exist Exits axe
axis axle exact ex libris exotic exiled

exempt exhaust Exodus exogamy: exempt::
x-ray; overtax overtaxed oxygen; Oxford
Ox: X marks the spot: extreme extremely

[Z]
[A]

[Z]

Zip [A] finger to [Z]

a aa aaa z zz zzz aa zz aa zz aaa zz aa
a aa aaa z zz zzz aa zz aa zz aaa zz aa

aazz aaqq aazz aaqq qaz zaq qaz azz zqq
aazz aaqq aazz aaqq qaz zaq qaz azz zqq

zzza aaaq qqqa aaaz zaqa azaq qaza aqzz
zzza aaaq qqqa aaaz zaqa azaq qaza aqzz

qqaazz zzaaqq qqzzaa aazzqq qaz zaq qaz
qqaazz zzaaqq qqzzaa aazzqq qaz zaq qaz

Words

Zebra Quiz Quizzes Quizzed Azores: Zest
ooze oozed oozes zygomatic Zealot Zaire
ZAP: zinc Aztec azalea azure maze amaze

matzo ball; maximize; hazards; buzzard;
Mazurka iodize oxidize Zeisler: Zimmer:
Zurich; Zeya; Zambia; Zab zoo doze daze

[N]
[J]

[N][M]

Zip [J] finger to [N]

j jj jjj m mm mmm j jj jjj n nn nnn jnj
j jj jjj m mm mmm j jj jjj n nn nnn jnj

jjmm jjnn jjmn jjnm mmnn jmnj nnjj jnmj
jjmm jjnn jjmn jjnm mmnn jmnj nnjj jnmj

Resumes and Cover Letters

Whether you're graduating from school or looking for a new job, you'll need to prepare a resume and cover letter.

What to include in your resume

If you're graduating and don't have much work experience in the field, start with a heading that says "Objectives" telling the prospective employer what you're looking for. If you're currently in the field, start with a heading that says "Professional Highlights" stating two or three of your key accomplishments. When you submit your resume online, start with a heading that says "Keywords" matching your skills with the skills the company is looking for. Include:

- Your work experience (in chronological order from the most current)
- Relevant courses (if you're graduating)
- Extracurricular activities (if you're graduating)
- Community service (if you're in the workforce)
- Awards or special recognition (if you're in the workforce)
- Education (with honors if you received any)

Note: If you're graduating, a one-page resume will be sufficient. If you have a lot of experience, a two-page resume will keep you from shortchanging your experience.

References

Don't include a list of references or mention that references are available on request. The latter is assumed. No one will check your references before they meet you to determine they're interested in learning more about you.

Cover letters

For every resume you send through the mail, include a one-page cover letter. For every resume you send electronically, include the same information in an email. Send the resume as an attachment.

Opening paragraph: State how you heard of the position.
Middle paragraph: Detail how your experiences can serve the company.
Closing paragraph: Request an interview.

EXERCISE 1

Sample Resume for Someone in the Workforce

Type the following two-page resume exactly as you see it.

```
jjhh jjuu jjmm jjnn jumn jhnm jjmmnn jn
jjhh jjuu jjmm jjnn jumn jhnm jjmmnn jn

jjmmjjm mmjjmmj jjnmjjn mjnm jmmj mnnjm
jjmmjjm mmjjmmj jjnmjjn mjnm jmmj mnnjm
```

Words
```
Nancy Nannette; ennoble enough narcotic
Nation; Indian: natron natural network:
response responsive responsiveness next

panniers staunches; Norton N. Nicholson
Nelson; niceness piano picnic; Jacobean
itinerant converts conversion announces
```

You have now learned the entire alphabet. Type it until you are comfortable with all the letters.

Alphabet
```
a b c d e f g h i j k l m n o p q r s t u v w x y z

ab cd ef gh ij kl mn op qr st uv wx yz
abc def ghi jkl mno pqr stu vwx yz

Aa Bb Cc Dd Ee Ff Gg Hh Ii Jj Kk Ll Mm
Nn Oo Pp Qq Rr Ss Tt Uu Vv Ww Xx Yy Zz
```

Index Fingers
Your index fingers type approximately 46 percent of the letters of the alphabet. Let's practice using your index fingers only.

```
fur gun gum fun hut hum but buy jut bug bun
fur gun gum fun hut hum but buy jut bug bun

guy hung hug bunt hunt gnu grunt fry guru
guy hung hug bunt hunt gnu grunt fry guru
```

6. Sarcasm and Humor

You should avoid sarcasm and humor in all business situations, but it's more critical when you're communicating with different cultures. Many points have been missed and international contacts lost due to the misunderstanding of humor.

7. Phone Numbers

Always provide proper international dialing codes and other contact information when sending emails overseas.

8. Monetary Translations

When mentioning currency, use either the currency of both countries or the currency of the country in which the financial dealings take place.

9. Measurements

Most countries use the metric system. It may be wise to show the American and metric equivalents. For example: 1 inch (25 millimeters).

Note: For more valuable information on business writing and email, check out my blog, *http://writing-ace.blogspot.com.*

It is time to check your progress once again. If you have not gotten much faster since the last module, do not worry. You are still very much in the learning stage.

about	beat	card	debit	enough	feisty	7
gamma	hard	ibis	knife	laughs	mister	14
newer	open	pins	quite	really	spouse	21
tried	unit	very	woman	xyloid	yearly	28
zebra	quit	want	paper	loiter	crayon	35

1   2   3   4   5   6   7

pencils	paper	scissors	glue	erasers		7
spinach	lettuce	radish	tomato	beans		14
comma	period	semicolon	quote	hyphen		21
New York	Arkansas	Washington	Kansas			28
dress	skirt	pants	blouse	scarf	ring	35

1   2   3   4   5   6   7

Rate Yourself

7 wpm = fair
14 wpm = good
21 wpm = very good
28 wpm = excellent
35 wpm = superior

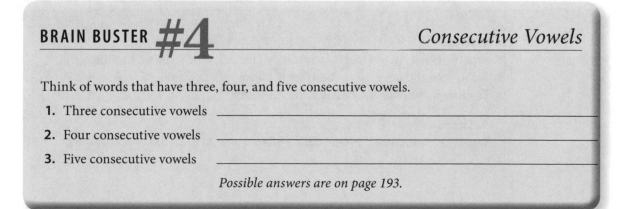

BRAIN BUSTER #4   *Consecutive Vowels*

Think of words that have three, four, and five consecutive vowels.

1. Three consecutive vowels _____

2. Four consecutive vowels _____

3. Five consecutive vowels _____

Possible answers are on page 193.

The following appears on my blog. Type it for practice.

Emails Across Cultures and Time Zones

Nine must-know tips for sending global emails that create goodwill and get results.

Email is a serious business communications tool and you must treat it with the same respect as any other business document you write—yet people don't. Here are nine must-know tips for sending emails across the world's cultures and time zones:

1. Formality
The friendliness of Americans can seem overbearing to people in many foreign countries. Therefore, always address people by their last names until you establish a relationship.

2. Tone
- Minimize abbreviations and acronyms. If you use them, explain them.
- Avoid slang and jargon.
- Use simple vocabulary and conventional syntax.
- Over-explain, rather than under-explain.

3. Time Sensitivities
Answer emails as soon as you can, but don't always expect the same in return. Your email may arrive during your recipient's off-work hours or on a holiday you don't know about. So, don't be in a rush to resend the same message or a follow-up.

4. Dates
When sending an international email that includes dates, be sure to translate using date and time conventions for the appropriate country. For example, in European countries March 2 would be 2 March.

5. Times
Most countries use a 24-hour clock. For example, 3 PM would be 1500 hours.

MODULE 4

Punctuation Marks

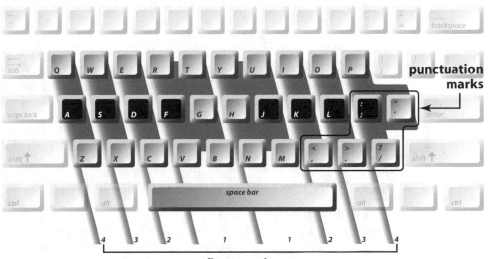

finger paths

Note: Keys are spaced apart to depict finger paths.

Now that you have learned the entire alphabet, it is time to type sentences. But what is a sentence without punctuation marks?

[;] You have already learned the semicolon. It is a home row key. Let's just practice.

Note Space once after a semicolon.

```
Atlanta, Georgia; Nyack, New York; Taos, New
Mexico; Dallas, Texas; Louisville, Kentucky;
San Francisco, California; Phoenix, Arizona;

Tuesday, January 9; Monday, April 3; Friday,
July 7; Thursday, November 9; Saturday, May,
20; Wednesday, February 8; Sunday, August 27
```

- I like red. I like blue. I like purple. (I like all three colors equally.)
- I like red. I like blue. And I like purple. (I'm saying that purple is my favorite of the three colors.)

Smile

Thank you and *please* are equivalent to a smile or friendly nod. If you exclude those words, especially in emails, you send a demanding message.

Respect personal space

Personal space is the invisible region around your body you don't want others to enter unless they're invited. One way to honor personal space in writing is to provide lots of white space. This includes 1"-to-1.5" margins on the top, bottom, and sides of paper documents; spacing between paragraphs; and spaces above and below bulleted and numbered lists.

Point

Bold, underscore, and italics "tell" the reader the text is important. If you were face to face, you'd point your finger to signify importance.

Expression tone

Use punctuation to project a dull mumble, a joyful expression, a neutral sound, or a shy whisper. Notice how punctuation changes the tone in the following sentences:

- The ABC Company—winner of the service award—just introduced its new product line. (The dashes heighten what's enclosed as if you're raising your voice.)
- The ABC Company (winner of the service award) just introduced its new product line. (The parentheses play down what's enclosed as if you're lowering your voice.)
- The ABC Company, winner of the service award, just introduced its new product line. (The commas neutralize what's enclosed.)

Copyright 2008. All rights reserved. http://www.sherylwrites.com

[.]
[L]
   ↘

     [.]

Zip [L] finger to [.]

```
l ll lll . .. ... ll.. ..ll l..l .ll. ll ...
l ll lll . .. ... ll.. ..ll l..l .ll. ll ...

lloo ll.. llo. ..lo ool. ll.. ...o ll.l ol..
lloo ll.. llo. ..lo ool. ll.. ...o ll.l ol..
```

Abbreviations

```
Dr. A.M.A. Jr. Sr. Mr. Mrs. Ms. Esq. St. Rd.
Ave. doz. lb. Inc. Ltd. Rev. Msgr. A.M. P.M.
B.A. B.S. M.A. M.S. M.B.A. Ph.D. e.g.; i.e.;
```

Sentences

Note Space once after a period at the end of a sentence.

```
Sam fed us. See Mr Doe. Lou asked for salad.
Bob sold all his dogs. Dale saw the cowboys.
He did. She did. Yes. Janice wrote a letter.

I have learned to type. He types quite well.
Eve used a computer. The ski slope is steep.
I like the color yellow. I also like purple.
```

[,]
[K]
   ↘

     [,]

Zip [K] finger to [,]

```
k kk kkk , ,, ,,, kk,, ,,kk k,,k ,kk, kk ,,,
k kk kkk , ,, ,,, kk,, ,,kk k,,k ,kk, kk ,,,

kkii kk,, kki, ,,ki iik, kk,, ,,,i kk,k ik,,
kkii kk,, kki, ,,ki iik, kk,, ,,,i kk,k ik,,
```

Words

Note Space once after a comma.

```
, happy, glad, mad, elated, Spanish, French,
Spanish, story, video, computer, television,
cereal, crackers, zesty, panic, work, works,
evenly, commas, comas, comes, type, end, , ,
```

Blogs

Blogs

Weblogs, or blogs, are websites that display postings by one or more people in chronological order. With just a few clicks, digital photos, PowerPoint presentations, emails, government reports, and more can be broadcast into the blogosphere. Blogging has grown into a completely new way of doing business. Bloggers share thoughts and ideas, foster personal relationships and communities, build personal and corporate credibility, and grab search-engine attention.

Use a blog to build your business

Whether you're a solo-preneur or a mid- or large-size company, a blog puts your name and your company "out there," as does a website. You can post and update a blog yourself without the help of a web developer. Blogging is an easy way to communicate with customers, clients, and employees. And when you launch a public relations campaign, treat bloggers as if they're the press.

EXERCISE 1

The following appears on my blog. Type it for practice.

Use "body language" in writing

Body language has been a source of interpersonal understanding since the beginning of the human race. Even when you're not speaking, you're communicating through your body language. Here are some ways to incorporate body language into your writing:

Shake hands
When you include salutations and closings in your emails, you extend a warm and friendly handshake. If you omit them, you send a cold and unfriendly message.

Accentuate words or phrases
Start a sentence with *and* or *but* to accentuate the words that follow. Look at the difference between the following sentences:

Sentences

Yes, he did. No, he will not. Try it, Ginny.
Please, Barbara. No, I cannot. Okay, I will.
Later, perhaps. Good, we can. Yes, tomorrow.

Okay, it is finished. No, it is not snowing.
Try it, Edward. Eat it, Susan. No, I cannot.
If it is, I will. However, I will see later.

[:]

The colon appears above the semicolon on a home row key. Leave your finger on the semicolon and press [Shift] with your pinkie to type a colon.

```
; ;; ;;; : :: ::: ;; :: ;;; ::: ;:; ::; ;;:;
; ;; ;;; : :: ::: ;; :: ;;; ::: ;:; ::; ;;:;
```

Words

Note

Space once after a colon.

Ladies: Gentlemen: Dear Ms. Smith: From: To:
Ladies and Gentlemen: the following: follow:

To Whom This May Concern: as follows: Mommy:
Dear Mr. Quincy: Dear Judge Williams: Hello:

Sentences

I like the following fruits: apples, grapes,
and strawberries.
The following names were listed: Mr. Matson,
Mrs. Kirk, and Ms. Fallon.
Please take the following: tent, stoves, and
matches.

[']

[;] → [']

Zip [;] finger to [']

```
; ;; ;;; ' '' ''' ; ;; ;;; ' '' ''' ; ;; ''
; ;; ;;; ' '' ''' ; ;; ;;; ' '' ''' ; ;; ''
```

Translate the following headlines into the names of commonly known movies, stories, or fairy tales and type the translations.

Example: Elderly Woman and Canine Pet Face Starvation = Old Mother Hubbard

1. Youngster Vanishes in Freak Storm

2. Couple Suffering From Dietary Allergies Reach Agreement

3. Poor Bargain Brings Ultimate Wealth

4. Friends Eager to Assist in Painting Project

5. Unique Individual Mortally Injured in Crash

6. Odd Pair Embarks on Ocean Voyage in Chartreuse Vehicle

7. Remote Country Home Vandalized by Blond

8. Browbeaten Girl Courted by Royal Heir

9. Friendless Waif Adopted by Group of Miners

10. Shepherdess Proves Derelict in Duty

Possible answers are on page 197.

Words

Note   Do not space after an apostrophe unless it ends a word.

```
won't can't didn't wasn't haven't hadn't A's
The Lanes' sister-in-law's dog's dogs' wit's
```

Sentences
```
Samuel Jones was at his wit's end yesterday.
The ladies' and men's locker rooms are here.
The Cohens' house is just across the street.

Their horses' stalls were cleaned yesterday.
The audience's reaction was very astounding.
The new children's books are in that corner.
```

["]   Zip [;] to ['] and press [Shift]

Help Menu   This key is commonly used for quoted material, but if necessary you should refer to your Help menu or user manual for instructions on how to type professional-looking quotation marks.

```
; ;; ;;  '  ' '  ' ' '  "  " "  " " "  ;;  ' '  " "  ; ' "  ; ' " "
; ;; ;;  '  ' '  ' ' '  "  " "  " " "  ;;  ' '  " "  ; ' "  ; ' " "
```

[?]
[;]
    ↘
    [?]

```
; ;; ;;; ? ?? ??? ;;?? ??;; ;??; ?;;? ;; ???
; ;; ;;; ? ?? ??? ;;?? ??;; ;??; ?;;? ;; ???
```

Words

Note   Space once after a question mark.

```
Who? How? Why? When? Did you? Did he? Maybe?
Can she? Why not? If not now, when? Did she?
Will she? Can we? Did they? Could they? Huh?
```

EMOTICONS

Emoticons are especially useful when you want to show your true meaning or intentions, such as when saying something in a joking way. They're more appropriate for personal use than for business.

Type the following emoticons using your phone or PDA.

:-)	Smile
:-@	Angry
:-(	Sad
:-S	Confused
:-$	Embarrassed
8-)	Rolling your eyes
:-O	Shouting
:-X	Lips are sealed
:-|	Expressionless
:-8	Screaming
]:-)>	Devilish
~&:-(	Having a bad hair day

Do you know? Did they ask? Will you ask her?
Does he think so? Why was he not also asked?

[/]

[;]

↘

[/]

Zip [;] finger to [/]

The virgule is known by many names, including *diagonal*, *solidus*, *oblique*, *slant*, *slash*, and *slash mark*. It's generally used to represent a word that is not written out or to separate or set off certain adjacent elements of text.

The virgule can also be used for computer applications, as in the *http://* used for World Wide Web addresses. It should not be confused with the back slash [\], used frequently in computer commands and file names.

; ;; ; ? ?? ??? / // /// ; // ??? ? ;; ///?/
; ;; ; ? ?? ??? / // /// ; // ??? ? ;; ///?/

Sentences

Note

Do not space after a virgule.

Send the package c/o Sally Reynolds.
The A/V room will open at nine tomorrow.
Ms. Smith and/or Mr. Jones will be there.
They estimated 40,000 tons/year.

The projectile traveled 9 ft/sec.
I received an I/O error on the computer.
What is the price/earnings ratio?
The article is in the May/June issue.
It was in 1990/91.
It is an innovative classroom/laboratory.

[-]

[-]

↗

[P]

↗

[;]

Zip [;] finger to [-] (This is a big Zip.)

; ;; - -- --- ; ;; ;;; p pp ppp - -- ---
; ;; - -- --- ; ;; ;;; p pp ppp - -- ---

SLAP Sounds like a plan
SN Screen name
SO Significant other
SYS See you soon

TAFN That's all for now
TBA To be announced
TBH To be honest
THX Thanks
TIA Thanks in advance
TTBOMK To the best of my knowledge
TTFN Ta ta for now
TTYL Talk to you later
TY Thank you

UN User Name

WB Welcome back
WE Whatever
WFM Works for me
WRT With respect to
WTG Way to go
WU? What's up?

YCQMOT You can quote me on this
YOYO You're on your own
YT? You there?
YW You're welcome
YWSYLS You win some, you lose some

Words

Note   Do not space after a hyphen.

mayor-elect write-in trade-in write-off
sister-in-law H-beam A-frame J-bar lift
off-season rates stick-to-itiveness A-C

Sentences   He just got a part-time job.
It was a very well-funded project.
The man next door is a jack-of-all-trades.

The president is a tough-minded negotiator.
The contract has an iron-clad guarantee.
Do not worry, it is a risk-free investment.

[!]   Zip [A] finger to [1] and press [Shift]
[!]

       [Q]   a aa aaa q qq qqq 1 11 ! !! !!! 11!! !!11
                a aa aaa q qq qqq 1 11 ! !! !!! 11!! !!11

       [A]   aaa qqq 111 !!! !!! 111 qqq aaa aq1 1qa!!
                aaa qqq 111 !!! !!! 111 qqq aaa aq1 1qa!!

Words

Note   Space once after an exclamation point.

No, no! Ugh! Fire! Stop! Stop that! Ouch!
Wow! Alas! The time is now! Eek! A mouse!
Wait! Absurd! Yes, yes! Get out! Not now!

Sentences   What an awful time we had!
Sh! The meeting has begun.
Psst! Come over here.

Ouch! That hurts.
Ugh! What a horrible taste.
Ah, those blue eyes!

IKWUM I know what you mean
I LV U I love you or I'm leaving you [quite a difference]
IM Instant message
IMHO In my humble opinion
IMNSHO In my not so humble opinion
IMO In my opinion
IMS I am sorry
IOW In other words

JIC Just in case
JK Just kidding
JTLYK Just to let you know

K Okay
KIS Keep it simple
KWIM Know what I mean?

L8R Later

MHBFU My heart bleeds for you
MYOB Mind your own business

NBD No big deal
NP No problem
NRN No response necessary

OBTW Oh, by the way
OH Off hand
OIC Oh I see
OTL Out to lunch
OTOH On the other hand
OTP On the phone

PMFJI Pardon me for jumping in
PLS *or* **PLZ** Please
POC Point of contact
POS Parent over shoulder
POV Point of view

ROTFL Rolling on the floor laughing
RSN Real soon now
RUOK? Are you okay?

[( )]   Zip [L] finger to [9] and press [Shift] for a left parenthesis.
[() ())]   Zip [;] finger to [0] and press [Shift] for a right parenthesis.

        ↖ ↖
    [0]   *[P]*
       ↖   ↖
      [L]   *[;]*

```
l ll lll o oo ooo 9 99 999 ( (( ((( lo9( (9ol
l ll lll o oo ooo 9 99 999 ( (( ((( lo9( (9ol

; ;; ;;; p pp ppp 0 00 000 ) )) ))) 0p;) )p;0
; ;; ;;; p pp ppp 0 00 000 ) )) ))) 0p;) )p;0
```

Words

Note   Do not space after a left parenthesis; space once after a right parenthesis.

```
(left) (right) (parentheses) (open) (close)
(not brackets) (wow) (big) (help) (enclose)
(shout) (he thought) (she wants) (wishful)
```

Sentences

```
Please call Evelyn (by telephone) tomorrow.
Please designate the exact Road (or Rd).
Antonyms (such as pro, con) are opposites.

Have you heard of Earl (Fatha) Hines?
I'll know more tomorrow (Friday).
The diagram (next page) illustrates that.
```

BG Big grin
BI Buddy icon
BL Buddy list
BMG Be my guest
BRB Be right back
BTA But then again
BTDT Been there, done that
BTW By the way

CFN Ciao for now
CID Consider it done
CSG Chuckle snicker grin
CTRN Can't talk right now
CUL *or* **CUL8R** See you later
CYL Catch you later

DHTB Don't have the bandwidth
DQMOT Don't quote me on this

EOM End of message

FAQ Frequently asked questions
FTF Face to face
FWIW For what it's worth
FYA For your amusement
FYI For your information

GAL Get a life
GL Good luck
GMTA Great minds think alike
GRA Go right ahead
GW Good work

HAND Have a nice day
H&K Hug and kiss
HT Hi there
HTH Hope this helps

IAC In any case
IAE In any event
IDK I don't know
IHMB I hate my boss
IK I know

It is time to check your progress once again. If you have not gotten much faster since the last module, do not worry. These are slightly more difficult.

```
Yes, she ordered the A/V equipment.        7
"How," he asked, "are you feeling?"        14
Kelly called her new mother-in-law.        21
Dan Jones ordered the following: an        28
ice-cream cone and a tuna sandwich.        35
```

```
1       2       3       4       5       6       7
```

```
He liked the blue Chevy in the lot.        7
Carol bought the red couch on sale.        14
Steve asked, "What were the costs?"        21
David received his M.B.A. from MIT.        28
He called her from Aspen, Colorado.        35
```

```
1       2       3       4       5       6       7
```

Rate Yourself

  7 wpm = fair
14 wpm = good
21 wpm = very good
28 wpm = excellent
35 wpm = superior

Because your thumb is the least dexterous part of your hand, it's particularly vulnerable to injury from over use. Here are some exercises the American Physical Therapy Association (APTA) recommends to help avoid the malady termed *thumbitis*:

- Tap each finger with the thumb of the same hand. Repeat 5 times.
- Alternate tapping the palm of your hand and the back of your hand against your thigh as quickly as you can. Repeat 20 times.
- Open your hands and spread your fingers as far apart as possible. Hold for 10 seconds and repeat 8 times.
- Fold your hands together, and turn your palms away from your body as you extend your arms forward. You should only feel a gentle stretch. Hold for 10 seconds and repeat 8 times.
- Fold your hands together, turn your palms away from your body, and extend your arms overhead. You should feel the stretch in your upper torso and shoulders to hand. Hold for 10 seconds and repeat 8 times.

Also, take a 15-minute break every hour and place a support on your lap so your wrists are not flexed or bent.

EXERCISE 1

ABBREVIATIONS

Don't overuse these abbreviations in your messages because your text may look like a bowl of alphabet soup. Here are some of the abbreviations you may see. Type them on your phone or PDA.

AAMOF As a matter of fact
AFAIK As far as I know
AFK Away from computer keyboard
AIM AOL Instant Messenger
AM Away Message
ASAP As soon as possible
A/S/L Age/Sex/Location
ATM At the moment

B Back
BBL Be back later
BBS Be back soon
BC Because
BCNU Be seein' you
BEG Big evil grin
BFN Bye for now
BFO Blinding flash of the obvious

The term *oxymoron* goes back to a Greek word that combines *oxus*, "sharp," and *moros*, "foolish," and means "pointedly foolish." Thus an oxymoron is a term that contradicts itself. Type each sentence and complete it, supplying the second word of a commonly used oxymoron.

Example: That went over like a lead <u>balloon.</u>

1. The music was recorded _____ in the studio.

2. The Democrats mounted loyal _____ to the bill.

3. The report showed a standard _____ of 15 percent.

4. Do you think our criminal _____ system is working?

5. She is a student _____ at Hawkins Elementary School.

6. We'll be using plastic _____ for the picnic.

7. Please arrange the files alphabetically; they are now in random _____.

8. That picture is awful. In fact, it's pretty _____.

9. Lincoln was alive during the Civil _____.

10. That happened last week; it's old _____.

The answers are on page 193.

Instant Messaging and Texting

Instant Messaging   Instant messaging (also known as *IMing*) is revolutionizing the way people communicate. IMing allows two or more Internet users to exchange messages rapidly in the manner of a spoken conversation. Messages are immediately displayed on the screens of all recipients in a chronological display. Many experts believe that IMing will eventually replace email as a key business communications tool.

Text messaging   Text messaging (commonly referred to as *texting*) is a quick, quiet, and easy way to send a person-to-person (P2P) message from your cell phone to someone else's cell phone, hand-held computer, pager, or email address. So when you're stuck in a meeting or you're at the library, you can stay in touch—silently.

It's all in the thumbs.   This is an actual keyboard configuration. You type with your thumbs. It's amazing how quickly you can do it with practice.

Note: If you're using a cell phone to send text messages, press the key until you get the desired letter. For example, to type the letter C, tap the key three times—once for A, twice for B, and thrice for C.

MODULE 5

Numbers and Symbols

When you type numbers, you have the option of using the numbers on the keyboard or those to the right of it on the numeric keypad. It is strictly your preference based on ease of use and/or speed. Please note, however, that there are no symbols over the numbers on the numeric keypad. This module will focus on the numbers on the keyboard and their associated symbols. For more information on the numeric keypad, please refer to Module 6.

When you want to type a symbol that appears above a number on the keyboard, press [Shift], just as you would for a capital letter. Keyboards usually include any or all of the following symbols:

!	exclamation mark
@	at
#	number
$	dollar(s)
%	percent
^	caret
&	ampersand
*	asterisk
=	equal sign
+	plus sign

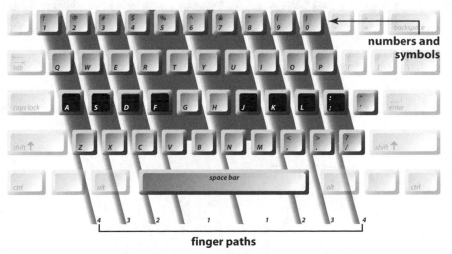

finger paths

Note: Keys are spaced apart to depict finger paths.

Reduce the following into commonly used expressions and type those expressions.

Example: A gyrating lithoidal fragment never accrues lichen. = A rolling stone gathers no moss.

1. Similar sire, similar scion.

2. Tenants of vitreous abodes ought not hurl lithoidal fragments.

3. It is not proper for mendicants to be indicative of preference.

4. It is fruitless to become lacrimatory because of scattered lacteal fluid.

5. Pulchritude does not extend below the surface of the derma.

6. Every article that is coruscated is not fashioned from aureate metal.

7. Freedom from guile or fraud constitutes the most excellent procedure.

8. Consolidated, you and I maintain ourselves; separated, we defer to the law of gravity.

9. You cannot estimate the contents of a bound printed narrative of record from the exterior vesture.

10. A feathered creature clasped in the manual member is equal in value to a brace in the bosky growth.

Possible answers are on page 196.

Many software programs provide characters that do not appear on the keyboard (i.e., digraphs, symbols, and diacriticals). These character sets must be supported by your printer in order to print on the hard copy.

[1]
[1]

[Q]

[A]

Zip [A] finger to [1]

```
a aa aaa q qq qqq 1 11 111aq1 1qa aq11
a aa aaa q qq qqq 1 11 111aq1 1qa aq11

111 qq aq1 11q aq1 11qqaa aaqq11 11qa1
111 qq aq1 11q aq1 11qqaa aaqq11 11qa1
```

[Shift] for [!]

Note

See Module 4 for more information about the exclamation mark. In this module, let's practice the [!] again.

```
a aa aaa q qq q11 ! !! !1! aq!! !qaq!!
a aa aaa q qq q11 ! !! !1! aq!! !qaq!!

11!! !!11 !1!1 aq1! !1qa aq1!! 1q1!A!!
11!! !!11 !1!1 aq1! !1qa aq1!! 1q1!A!!

Wow! How! Alas! I have 1 cent! Great!!
Wow! How! Alas! I have 1 cent! Great!!

Look out below! Fantastic! Wonderful!!
Look out below! Fantastic! Wonderful!!
```

[2]
[2]

[W]

[S]

Zip [S] finger to [2]

```
s ss sss w ww www 2 22 222sw2 2ws sw22
s ss sss w ww www 2 22 222sw2 2ws sw22

222 wsw 22wsw2 22ws sw2 2ws ww22 22ws2
222 wsw 22wsw2 22ws sw2 2ws ww22 22ws2
```

Type the following email message. Take note of the following inclusions:

- Salutation and closing
- Signature block
- Disclaimer

Dear Pavlova,

Please put an X through the section you want to delete. Put your initials next to that paragraph and return it to me. I'll take care of the rest. Thanks for bringing this to my attention.

My best,
Jeannie

Jeannie Smith
212.345.5565

The information transmitted in this electronic communication is intended only for the person or entity to whom it is addressed and may contain confidential and/or privileged material. Any review, retransmission, dissemination or other use of or taking of any action in reliance upon this information by persons or entities other than the intended recipient is prohibited. If you received this information in error, please contact the Compliance HelpLine at 800-834-3456 and properly dispose of this information.

[Shift] for [@]

```
s  ss  sss  w  ww  www  @  @@  @@@  @sw@@  @ws@@
s  ss  sss  w  ww  www  @  @@  @@@  @sw@@  @ws@@

2  22  22  @  @@  @@  22@@  sw2@@  w@@sw  sw2@@
2  22  22  @  @@  @@  22@@  sw2@@  w@@sw  sw2@@

1  @12  2  @  12  11  @  22  12  @  12.2  1  @  1.2
1  @12  2  @  12  11  @  22  12  @  12.2  1  @  1.2

Invoice 121, 2 pieces @ 12 cents each.
Invoice 121, 2 pieces @ 12 cents each.
```

[3]
[3]

[E]

[D]

Zip [D] finger to [3]

```
d  dd  ddd  e  ee  eee  3  33  333  de3  33ed  d3
d  dd  ddd  e  ee  eee  3  33  333  de3  33ed  d3

de3  3ed  de33  33ed  d33de  33ed3  3ede3  33
de3  3ed  de33  33ed  d33de  33ed3  3ede3  33
```

[Shift] for [#]

```
d  dd  ddd  e  ee  eee  #  ##  ###  de33##  #3ed
d  dd  ddd  e  ee  eee  #  ##  ###  de33##  #3ed

d##e  de3##  #3eed  de3#  dee3#d  de3  3E##d
d##e  de3##  #3eed  de3#  dee3#d  de3  3E##d

#123  #321  #331  #2  #2112  #321  #221  #231
#123  #321  #331  #2  #2112  #321  #221  #231

The numbers were #1, #22, #3, and #23.
The numbers were #1, #22, #3, and #23.
```

Type the following email message. Take note of the following inclusions:

- Salutation and closing
- Underscored headlines
- Signature block
- Tagline

Hi Cynthia,

I hope you had a pleasant summer, one with lots of fun in the sun. Sorry for this late notice on the classes, but this has been a very busy time. Classes run for six weeks starting on Monday, May 5, and Tuesday, May 6. Here's the new schedule:

<u>Mondays</u>
Mornings: 9:30 – 11:30
Afternoons: 12:30 – 2:30

<u>Tuesdays</u>
Mornings: 9:00 – 11:00
Afternoons: 12:00 – 2:00

Please let me know which date and time will work for you. Thanks.

Have a great weekend,
Madison

Madison Eisley
404.564.2245

We train—You gain!

[4]
[4]

[R]

[F]

Zip [F] finger to [4]

```
f ff fff r rr rr 4 44 44 fr4 44rf fr44
f ff fff r rr rr 4 44 44 fr4 44rf fr44

fr4 44r fr44 44rf fr4 4rff ffrr44 44rf
fr4 44r fr44 44rf fr4 4rff ffrr44 44rf
```

[Shift] for [$]

```
f ff fff r rr rrr $ $$ $$$ fr$$ $$rf $
f ff fff r rr rrr $ $$ $$$ fr$$ $$rf $

44$$ $r4$$ fr4$$ $r4f4 $rfr $$rf r44r$
44$$ $r4$$ fr4$$ $r4f4 $rfr $$rf r44r$

I gave $1.22, $2.13, $4.32, and $3.21.
I gave $1.22, $2.13, $4.32, and $3.21.

$3.22, $421.23, $234.12, $44.32, $2.43
$3.22, $421.23, $234.12, $44.32, $2.43
```

[5]
[5]

[R]

[F]

Zip [F] finger to [5]

```
f ff fff r rr rrr 5 55 555 fr5 5tf f55
f ff fff r rr rrr 5 55 555 fr5 5tf f55

fr5 tfg fr5 55rf r55 5tf ffr5 55rf 55r
fr5 tfg fr5 55rf r55 5tf ffr5 55rf 55r
```

[Shift] for [%]

```
fff rrr 555% %%rr 5rrf 5% ft%r fg%% 5%
fff rrr 555% %%rr 5rrf 5% ft%r fg%% 5%

45% ft5 554 f4 234 41g fr5 %%f f4% 44%
45% ft5 554 f4 234 41g fr5 %%f f4% 44%
```

Type the following email message. Take note of the following inclusions:

- Salutation and closing
- Bulleted list
- Signature block

Note: When using bulleted or numbered lists, always leave a line space above and below.

Hi Joe,

I'm attaching the materials for the workshop scheduled for October 1. Here are a few instructions:

* The file worksheets.doc contains all the worksheets for the program.
* The file cover.doc is the cover. Please attach it to the worksheets. You don't have to copy any of these in color. B&W will suffice.
* Don't collate the before.doc and after.doc files. Keep them in two separate files.

Please let me know if you have any questions. I look forward to seeing you on October 1.

Best regards,
Anna

Anna Sinn, President
AS & Associates
617.654.4456
www.as_associates.com

25% 45% He scored 11%. 43% 32% 11% %%5
25% 45% He scored 11%. 43% 32% 11% %%5

Sheldon told us 55%, 32%, 12%, and 1%.
Sheldon told us 55%, 32%, 12%, and 1%.

Practice

1!! 2@@@ 33## saw!! @123 #213 we! see!
1!! 2@@@ 33## saw!! @123 #213 we! see!
$432.23 fr$$ #432 Fred! fast! @2.34 !!
$432.23 fr$$ #432 Fred! fast! @2.34 !!

#321 2 @ 34 dqs!! !@##@! qwe!asd 1s#@3
#321 2 @ 34 dqs!! !@##@! qwe!asd 1s#@3
45% 12% $15.54 Wow! 5@ 25 cents ft%3!!
45% 12% $15.54 Wow! 5@ 25 cents ft%3!!

Wow! Jackie spent $43.14 on groceries.
The bananas were priced: 2 @ 50 cents.
Pay these invoices: #4, #23, and #135.
His percentages were 2%, 24%, and 45%.

[6]
[6]

[Y]

[J]

Zip [J] finger to [6]

j jj jjj y yy yyy 6 66 666 jy6 6yj j66
j jj jjj y yy yyy 6 66 666 jy6 6yj j66

jy6 6yj jy6 66yj j6 66y jy66 6yjy6 6yj
jy6 6yj jy6 66yj j6 66y jy66 6yjy6 6yj

[Shift] for [^]

66^^ 6^6^ jy^^ ^yjy6^^Y y hjy 6^^ jy^^
66^^ 6^6^ jy^^ ^yjy6^^Y y hjy 6^^ jy^^

6y^ jhy6^^ ^yjh ^^jj^^ ^yh jy6 jy^ 6yh
6y^ jhy6^^ ^yjh ^^jj^^ ^yh jy6 jy^ 6yh

Type the following email message. Take note of the following inclusions:

- Salutation and closing
- Underscored key information
- Bold sidelines
- Signature block

Hi Jane, Pat, and Sam,

We hope to go live with our new website within the next two months, so we must get going quickly. <u>Attendance is mandatory</u> at this meeting.

     Date: June 15, 20—
     Time: Noon (We'll be providing lunch.)
     Place: Conference Room 405

<u>Next step</u>
If this date doesn't work for you, please let me know by June 1 so we can reschedule.

Thanks,
Bill

Bill Smith
Bill Smith Enterprises
508.345.5566
www.billsmith.com

She told me she would use the ^. When?
She told me she would use the ^. When?
0, Bugs Bunny and Peter Rabbit eat ^^?
0, Bugs Bunny and Peter Rabbit eat ^^?

[7]
[7]

[U]

[J]

Zip [J] finger to [7]

j jj jjjj u uu uuu 7 77 777 ju7 7uj j7
j jj jjjj u uu uuu 7 77 777 ju7 7uj j7

hu7 77uj ju7 7uj uu7 77u ju77 777 7ju7
hu7 77uj ju7 7uj uu7 77u ju77 777 7ju7

[Shift] for [&]

7 77 777 & && &&& ju7 77u &&u j7& 7&uj
7 77 777 & && &&& ju7 77u &&u j7& 7&uj

77 && 7&&7 ju7 7u jj77 77&& &&jj ju77&
77 && 7&&7 ju7 7u jj77 77&& &&jj ju77&

This & that. His & hers. Yours & mine.
This & that. His & hers. Yours & mine.

This & that & the other thing. 14 & 27
This & that & the other thing. 14 & 27

[8]
[8]

[I]

[K]

Zip [K] finger to [8]

k kk kkk i ii iii 8 88 888 88 ii kk i8
k kk kkk i ii iii 8 88 888 88 ii kk i8

ki8 8ik kkii 88ik ki8 888 8ik kki8 8ik
ki8 8ik kkii 88ik ki8 888 8ik kki8 8ik

Rules of thumb for typing emails:

- Never use all capital letters.
- Never use all lowercase.
- Use proper punctuation.

In the following exercise, type the message in upper- and lowercase and insert the correct punctuation.

> DEAR PAT I WANT A MAN WHO KNOWS WHAT LOVE IS ALL ABOUT YOU ARE GENEROUS KIND THOUGHTFUL PEOPLE WHO ARE NOT LIKE YOU ADMIT TO BEING USELESS AND INFERIOR YOU HAVE RUINED ME FOR OTHER MEN I YEARN FOR YOU I HAVE NO FEELINGS WHATSOEVER WHEN WE'RE APART I CAN BE HAPPY FOREVER WILL YOU LET ME BE YOURS CHRIS

Here are a few possible ways for you to have typed this message:

A warm and caring message

> Dear Pat,
>
> I want a man who knows what love is all about. You are generous, kind, thoughtful. People who are not like you admit to being useless and inferior. You have ruined me for other men. I yearn for you. I have no feelings whatsoever when we're apart. I can be happy forever. Will you let me be yours?
>
> Chris

A cold and distant message

> Dear Pat,
>
> I want a man who knows what love is. All about you are generous, kind, thoughtful people who are not like you. Admit to being useless and inferior. You have ruined me. For other men I yearn. For you I have no feelings whatsoever. When we're apart I can be happy forever. Will you let me be?
>
> Yours,
>
> Chris

[Shift] for [*]

```
8 88 888 * ** *** kk ii 88 88ik* **ik*
8 88 888 * ** *** kk ii 88 88ik* **ik*

ki8 8** 8I K*K ki88** *iki8* *kKi8 II8
ki8 8** 8I K*K ki88** *iki8* *kKi8 II8

The ** asterisk ** looks like a star.
The ** asterisk ** looks like a star.

* This is the first item in the list.
* This is the second item in the list.
```

[9]
[9]

↖

[0]

↖

[L]

Zip [L] finger to [9]

```
l ll lll o oo ooo 9 99 999 lo9 99o ll9
l ll lll o oo ooo 9 99 999 lo9 99o ll9

l9 99ol lo9o llo9 99o 999 oll9 99o llo
l9 99ol lo9o llo9 99o 999 oll9 99o llo
```

[Shift] for [(]

Note

See Module 4 for more information about the opening parenthesis. In this module, let's practice the [(] again.

```
(9(9 lo(( (olo9((o llo9 9ool (olo9( 99
(9(9 lo(( (olo9((o llo9 9ool (olo9( 99

( is half a parentheses. It is lonely!
( is half a parentheses. It is lonely!

( is searching for its other half.((((
( is searching for its other half.((((
```

Write a compelling subject line. There are people who get hundreds of email messages a day, and they can't possibly read them all. If your subject line doesn't compel readers, they may never open your message. If you look down the subject line column of your inbox, perhaps you see subject lines such as these that give you absolutely no information and no reason to read the message:

> Billing
> Two things…
> About Brian
> Update

Always include in your subject line a key piece of information so your reader can get the gist of your message at a glance. Notice the following sets of subject lines and how much more compelling the second one (→) is.

> Profit report → 15% profit expected for Q2
> Sales meeting → Rescheduling 5/5 sales mtg to 5/6 at 2:30
> Contact you requested → Contact Jane Brown at Mellows Co.
> June 5 → Deadline moved to June 5
> Possible dates → Would July 6, 7, or 8 work?
> New hire → Brad Jones joining Mktg. Grp. April 5
> About Mark → Mark Jones still interested, but not ready to sign

Strive to write a subject line that's akin to a newspaper headline, giving readers information at a glance.

Replying to messages

When you reply to someone's message, change the subject line. To maintain continuity in a stream of messages, use a key word in the subject line and add the change to the message.

> Billing issues: To be discussed at April mtg.

Note: Email software typically defaults to an Arial font, which is easier to read on a computer screen than any serif font (such as Times Roman).

[0]
[0]

[P]

[;]

Zip [;] finger to [0]

```
; ;; ;;; p pp ppp 0 00 000 ;;p0 0p; p0
; ;; ;;; p pp ppp 0 00 000 ;;p0 0p; p0

00ol loO Op ;;p0 00p; ;;p0 Op;;p 00p;;
00ol loO Op ;;p0 00p; ;;p0 Op;;p 00p;;
```

[Shift] for [)]

Note

See Module 4 for more information about the closing parenthesis. In this module, let's practice the [)] again.

```
0 00 000 ) )) ))) p 00p0);p0)) 00p ;;p
0 00 000 ) )) ))) p 00p0);p0)) 00p ;;p

00 00p;; pp;0)) ))p;p0 00p;; ppOp; ppO
00 00p;; pp;0)) ))p;p0 00p;; ppOp; ppO

) is the other half of the parentheses.
When you type ), ( is no longer lonely.

Barbara (my sister) is standing there.
Barbara (my sister) is standing there.

(1) apple, (2) bananas, and (3) pears.
(1) apple, (2) bananas, and (3) pears.
```

[-]

[-]

[P]

[L]

Zip [l] finger to [-]

Note

See Module 4 for more information on the hyphen. In this module, let's practice the [-] again.

Email

Email is a serious business communications tool, and you should treat it with the same respect as any other business document you write. Just because the computer screen doesn't have the weft and feel of a sheet of paper, that's no excuse to abandon the good habits you learned for the print medium.

Do's

1. Respond within 24 hours.
2. Use the auto-response feature when you'll be away from the office and won't be checking messages.
3. When returning from a trip, review your messages from the most current to the least current.
4. Change the subject line when you reply to a message.
5. Use salutations and closings.
6. Include a signature block with your name and contact information.
7. Provide ample white space.
8. Limit paragraphs to about 8 lines of text.
9. Use *To*, *Cc*, and *Bcc* appropriately.
10. Be cautious of sending attachments; they must be in a format people can read and in a size they can receive.
11. Praise through email; give constructive criticism verbally.
12. Delete trailers unless you need them for a specific reason.

Taboos

1. Responding to "All" unless it's absolutely necessary.
2. Rambling. Ask yourself the *who, what, when, where, why*, and *how* questions your reader will ask and need answered.
3. Sending Rambograms—anything rude, crude, or lewd.
4. Putting too many disparate thoughts in one message.
5. Assuming the recipient actually received (read) your message.
6. Using too casual a tone.
7. Using work email for personal business.
8. Using *yesterday, today*, or *tomorrow*. They're relative to when the recipient reads the message, not to when you send it.

Just a reminder: The top of the hyphen key has the underscore character. On a computer, however, you cannot underscore a character using the underscore key. If you need to underscore, use the underscore feature of the software, not the key.

```
sister-in-law, seventy-three, off-line
sister-in-law, seventy-three, off-line
editor-in-chief, twenty-one, 1993-1994
editor-in-chief, twenty-one, 1993-1994

pages 89-146, two-thirds, self-control
pages 89-146, two-thirds, self-control
on-line, part-time job, Marlow-Ferrino
on-line, part-time job, Marlow-Ferrino
```

[=]

      [=]

     ↗

   [[]

 ↗

[;]

Zip [;] finger to [=]

```
; ;; ;;; [ [[ [[[ = == === ;[= =[; ;==
; ;; ;;; [ [[ [[[ = == === ;[= =[; ;==

===[[[[ ;;[[ ;[= ==[; ;;[= =[;;[==[;;=
===[[[[ ;;[[ ;[= ==[; ;;[= =[;;[==[;;=
```

[Shift] for [+]

```
= == === + ++ +++ ;[=++ ++====[[;[[ =+=
= == === + ++ +++ ;[=++ ++====[[;[[ =+=

3 + 5 = 6 Oops! No! 3 + 5 = 8 Better!!
3 + 5 = 6 Oops! No! 3 + 5 = 8 Better!!

1020+1000=2020, 653 + 200 = 853 Right?
1020+1000=2020, 653 + 200 = 853 Right?
```

Practice

```
1 2 3 4 5 6 7 8 9 0 9 8 7 6 5 4 3 2 1
1 2 3 4 5 6 7 8 9 0 9 8 7 6 5 4 3 2 1

2 4 6 8 10 2 4 6 8 10 2 4 6 8 10 even
2 4 6 8 10 2 4 6 8 10 2 4 6 8 10 even
```

Type the following sentences correctly:

Example: The passive voice should rarely be used. = Rarely use the passive voice.

1. Some say to never split an infinitive.

2. A verb should agree with their subject.

3. Proofread carefully to see if words left out repeated.

4. A writer shouldn't shift their point of view.

5. If any word is inproper at the end of a sentence, a linking verb is.

6. Take the bull by the horn and never mix metaphors.

7. Always pick on the correct idiom.

8. In general, a preposition isn't a word you should end a sentence with.

9. Give consideration to shortening long sentences by means of deleting unnecessary words.

10. Last, but not least, avoid clichés like the plague; seek viable alternatives.

Possible answers are on page 196.

```
1 3 5 7 9 1 3 5 7 9 1 3 5 7 9 all odd
1 3 5 7 9 1 3 5 7 9 1 3 5 7 9 all odd
```

He lives at 23 Main Street in Chicago.
Jane spent $125.55 on her school ring.
Michael Wasserman's Zip Code is 10243.
He will leave on September 15 at 2:00.

She had 5 pennies, 3 nickels, 7 dimes,
45 quarters, and 10 silver dollars. Do
you know how much that =? It = $22.15.

Charles is (1) tall, (2) dark, and (3)
handsome. And he got 100% on his test.
On December 1, he paid Gloria $500.00.
John's phone number is (508) 745-3213.

Jack's plane will leave from gate #35.
Invoice #456 (n/30) is due on the 1st.
$1,150.75 represents a savings of 50%.
Pat's picture frame measured 18 by 12.

Progress Check   It is time to check your progress once again. Numbers are more difficult than letters, so do not be discouraged if you slowed down slightly.

On October 14, 654 people attended.	7
June 20 marks our 15th anniversary.	14
She was given $5.00 to buy a dress.	21
Kate (my mother) is wearing purple.	28
Did I hear you say it was just 50%?	35

```
1     2     3     4     5     6     7
```

Proofreaders' Marks

Instruction	Mark in Margin	Mark on Proof	Corrected Type
GENERAL			
delete	⟆	the ~~best~~ word	the word
delete and close up space	⟆	the wo(r)rd	the word
insert indicated material	best	the ‸word	the best word
let it stand	(stet)	the best word	the best word
spell out	(sp)	(2) words	two words
POSITION AND SPACING			
new paragraph	¶	"Where is it?" / "It's on the shelf."	"Where is it?" "It's on the shelf."
flush paragraph	[¶	"Where is it?" / "It's on the shelf."	"Where is it?" "It's on the shelf."
transpose	(tr)	the word best	the best word
move left	[	[the word	the word
move right	]	]the word	the word
move down	⊔	the word	the word
move up	⊓	the word	the word
align	||	|| the word the word	the word the word
straighten line	=	the word	the word
insert space	#	the‸word	the word
equalize space	(eq #)	the‸best‸word	the best word
close up	⁀	the wo rd	the word
en space	◻ N	‸the word	the word
em space	◻ M	‸the word	the word
PUNCTUATION			
period	⊙	This is the word‸	This is the word.
comma	‸,	words‸words, words	words, words, words
hyphen	=‸	word‸for‸word test	word-for-word test
colon	(:)	The following words‸	The following words:
semicolon	;‸	Scan the words/skim the words.	Scan the words; skim the words.
apostrophe	∨	Johns words	John's words
double quotation marks	“/”	the word word	the word "word"
single quotation marks	‘/’	the "good word"	the "good 'word'"
parentheses	(/)	The list of words in the dictionary‸on page 101‸ is useful.	The list of words in the dictionary (on page 101) is useful.
brackets	[/]	He read the list of words ‸from the dictionary‸	He read the list of words [from the dictionary].
en dash	1/N	1984‸1992	1984–1992
em dash	1/M	The dictionary‸how often it is needed‸ belongs in every home.	The dictionary—how often it is needed—belongs in every home.
asterisk	∨*	word∨	word*
dagger	∨†	word‸	word†
virgule (slash)	/	either/or	either/or
three ellipses	/⊙/⊙/⊙/	the‸word	the...word
four ellipses	⊙/⊙/⊙/⊙/	the word‸	the word....
STYLE OF TYPE			
uppercase	(uc)	the word	The Word
lowercase	(lc)	The Word	the word
small capitals	(sc)	the word	THE WORD
italic	(ital)	the entry word	the entry *word*
roman	(rom)	the entry *word*	the entry word
boldface	(bf)	the entry word	the entry **word**
lightface	(lf)	**the entry word**	the entry word
wrong font	(wf)	the entry word	the entry word
superscript	∨2	22=4	2^2=4
subscript	‸2	H2O	H_2O

```
She lives at 204 5th Avenue, Salem.        7
Invoice #694 has a balance of $228.       14
Wow! $1,000 is certainly wonderful!       21
Mary was here & there & everywhere.       28
Two gold ** for the one who has it.       35

   1      2      3      4      5      6      7
   _____
```

Rate Yourself   7 wpm = fair
                  14 wpm = good
                  21 wpm = very good
                  28 wpm = excellent
                  35 wpm = superior

BRAIN BUSTER #6   *Letter Perfect*

Each equation contains the initials of words that will complete the expression. Type the complete expression.

Example: 24 = h. in a d. This stands for: 24 = hours in a day

   1. 26 = l. in the a.

   2. 1,001 = A.N.

   3. 12 = s. of the z.

   4. 5,280 = f. in a m.

   5. 88 = k. on a p.

   6. 13 = s. on the A.f.

   7. 32 = d. at which w.f.

   8. 90 = d. in a r.a.

   9. 8 = s. on a s.s.

   10. 4 = q. in a g.

Possible answers are on page 194.

February 30, 20—   ?

Acme Equipment Company
(SP) 24 Longfellow Rd.
(#) Detroit, MI 48256
(#) Dear Sir: ___ [Ladies or Gentlemen:
The maintainance of a good credit rating is vital
to any bussinesman person when your indebtness exceeds
your usual credit limit, you're in danger of
loosing the good credit standing you've recieved in
the passed past.
(#) ___ I am very sorry to have to right write you this
letter but I find that we have aloud allowed your
indebtness of $1,788.00 to continue much too long.
Unless payment in full is recieved within two
weeks from the date of this letter, you you will
leave us with no alternatives but to turn this
matter over to are our attorney.

Very Truly Yours,

Miss B. Haven

MODULE 6

Numeric Keypad

Most keyboards have a numeric keypad to the right enabling you to input numerals at high speeds. (Of course, for us "lefties" that takes some getting used to.) If you practice a lot and master the numeric keypad, you might be able to key in 200 digits per minute (dpm). The industry standard is 250 dpm.

The arrangement of the numerals will be the same from one keyboard to another, but the surrounding keys can vary. This is an example of a numeric keypad.

The following is an explanation of the surrounding keys.

[Num Lock]	Toggle [Num Lock] on and off. When it is on, you will be using the numbers; when it is off, you will be using the other markings on the keys.
[/] [*] [–] [+]	Mathematical functions: divide, multiply, subtract, add.
[Enter]	Same as [Enter] on the keyboard.
[Del]	Delete data.
[Ins]	Toggle between insert mode and overstrike mode.
Note	The home row is [4] [5] [6]. Your index finger will be placed on the 4; the middle finger, on the 5; and the ring finger, on the 6.

The following show marked-up versions of Exercises 3 and 4.

Feb**r**uary 3̶0̶, 20—

Mr. and Mrs. Frank N. Stein
14 Ivy Lane
Atlanta, GA 30303

Dear Mr. and Mrs. Stein**:**

Welcome to Atlanta!

Georgia It**'**s a pleasure to welcome you and your family to
Atlanta—the Peachtree State. To help you get to know
this wonderful area, we've enclosed a map of the
re**c**reational and cultural attractions in and around
Atlanta. Here are some of the highlights:

1. Georgia State Capit**o**l
2. Peachtree Center
3. Tullie Smith House
4. Martin Luther King, Jr., Historic District
5. Stone Mtn. Park   (Sp)

And while you**'re** getting to **k**now the city, stop by the
Georgia State Bank so **we** may welcome you personally and
share many of the wonderful experiences you can have
banking with us. Georgia State Bank is celebrating
its 15th anniversary and is sending you a̶s̶ a $10
gift certificate to start a savings account to help us
celebrate.

Sincerely **Y**ours,

Al Catraz
Branch Manager

Turn on [Num Lock]

Home Row Keys

[4] [5] [6]

4 44 444 4444 5 55 555 5555 6 66 666 6666
4 44 444 4444 5 55 555 5555 6 66 666 6666

4 44 555 6666 5 55 666 4444 5 55 555 6666
4 44 555 6666 5 55 666 4444 5 55 555 6666

456 456 4456 4456 4556 4556 4566 4566 456
456 456 4456 4456 4556 4556 4566 4566 456

44 55 66 44 55 66 66 55 44 55 66 44 44 55
44 55 66 44 55 66 66 55 44 55 66 44 44 55
56 45 65 45 56 44 56 64 45 56 64 45 65 44
55 66 65 54 45 56 45 65 45 65 45 55 66 45

Top Row Keys

[7]
[7]
↑
[4]

Zip [4] finger to [7]

4 44 444 7 77 777 44 77 444 777 47 74 477
4 44 444 7 77 777 44 77 444 777 47 74 477

7 777 774 44 44 747 447 774 447 774 44777
7 777 774 44 44 747 447 774 447 774 44777

45 56 67 76 65 45 47 65 47 75 67 77 74 56
45 56 67 76 65 45 47 65 47 75 67 77 74 56

4567 7654 456 667 675 457 776 765 456 774
4567 7654 456 667 675 457 776 765 456 774
7765 7654 456 777 667 775 774 675 675 745
7765 7654 456 777 667 775 774 675 675 745

Feburay 30, 20—

Acme Equiptment Company
24 Longfellow Rd.
Detroit, MI 48256
Dear Sir:
The maintainance of a good credit rating is vital
to any bussinesman.When you indebtness excedes
your usual credit limit, your in danger of
loosing the good credit standing youve recieved in
the passed.

I am very sorry to have to right you this
letter but I find that we have aloud your
indebtness of $1,788.00 to continue much to long.
UNless payment in full is recieved within two
weeks from the date of this letter, you you will
leave us with no alternative, but to turn this
matter over to are attorney.

Very Truly Yours,

Miss B. Haven

[8]
[8]
↑
[5]

Zip [5] finger to [8]

5 55 555 8 88 888 55 88 555 888 58 85 588
5 55 555 8 88 888 55 88 555 888 58 85 588

8 888 885 55 55 858 558 885 558 885 55888
8 888 885 55 55 858 558 885 558 885 55888

88 78 65 86 46 87 48 78 56 78 85 48 76 78
88 78 65 86 46 87 48 78 56 78 85 48 76 78

5588 8855 5886 8765 788 5678 8765 6788 78
5588 8855 5886 8765 788 5678 8765 6788 78
5678 8658 7788 8764 488 8678 8756 8766 68
5678 8658 7788 8764 488 8678 8756 8766 68

[9]
[9]
↑
[6]

Zip [6] finger to [9]

6 66 666 9 99 999 66 99 999 666 69 69 699
6 66 666 9 99 999 66 99 999 666 69 69 699

9 99 998 996 986 9586 695 559 994 458 965
9 99 998 996 986 9586 695 559 994 458 965

98 98 59 58 79 69 69 94 67 86 58 75 69 74
98 98 59 58 79 69 69 94 67 86 58 75 69 74

4685 6998 4896 5879 879 5879 8996 6654 79
4685 6998 4896 5879 879 5879 8996 6654 79
6998 5479 9658 9745 499 9657 7486 6589 96
6998 5479 9658 9745 499 9657 7486 6589 96

Bottom Row Keys

[1]
[4]
↓
[1]

Zip [4] finger to [1]

4 44 444 1 11 111 41 14 4411 1114 414 114
4 44 444 1 11 111 41 14 4411 1114 414 114

Exercises 3 and 4 contain errors. Use proofreaders' marks to identify each error. Then type each exercise correctly. (The marked-up versions are on pages 145–146.)

EXERCISE 3

Febuary 30, 20—

Mr. and Mrs. Frank N. Stein
14 Ivy Lane
Atlanta, GA 30303

Dear Mr. and Mrs. Stein,

Welcome to Atlanta!

Its a pleasure to welcome you and your family to Atlanta—the Peachtree State. To help you get to know this wonderful area, we've enclosed a map of the re-creational and cultural attractions in and around Atlanta. Here are some of the highlights:

1. Georgia State Capital
2. Peachtree Center
3. Tullie Smith House
4. Martin Luther King, Jr., Historic District
5. Stone Mtn. Park

And while your getting to now the city, stop by the Georgia State Bank so I may welcome you personally and share many of the wonderful experiences you can have banking with us. Georgia State Bank is celebrating their 15th anniversary and is sending you as a $10 gift certificate to start a savings account to help us celebrate.

Sincerely Yours,

Al Catraz,
Branch Manager

147 741 117 741 158 745 587 117 119 81 14
147 741 117 741 158 745 587 117 119 81 14

14 14 87 59 69 54 11 17 91 47 96 64 41 47
14 14 87 59 69 54 11 17 91 47 96 64 41 47

1459 5591 1471 1595 991 1185 6971 4759 91
1459 5591 1471 1595 991 1185 6971 4759 91
5681 9119 1475 5415 199 5874 5511 5698 69
5681 9119 1475 5415 199 5874 5511 5698 69

[2]
[5]
↓
[2]

Zip [5] finger to [2]

5 55 555 2 22 222 52 25 52 225 552 225 52
5 55 555 2 22 222 52 25 52 225 552 225 52

252 258 852 215 526 254 254 225 85 219 65
252 258 852 215 526 254 254 225 85 219 65

22 55 88 84 52 15 95 65 72 25 96 65 47 95
22 55 88 84 52 15 95 65 72 25 96 65 47 95

1599 6526 625 521 4581 9612 5796 2695 472
1599 6526 625 521 4581 9612 5796 2695 472
6952 2596 148 256 2698 2254 4425 5692 224
6952 2596 148 256 2698 2254 4425 5692 224

[3]
[6]
↓
[3]

Zip [6] finger to [3]

6 66 666 3 33 333 6 66 3 33 63 36 63 3336
6 66 666 3 33 333 6 66 3 33 63 36 63 3336

369 963 369 553 2596 325 32 3596 3214 477
369 963 369 553 2596 325 32 3596 3214 477

36 36 51 98 92 43 34 82 15 96 35 74 15 63
36 36 51 98 92 43 34 82 15 96 35 74 15 63

Temporary Agencies

Temporary agencies exist for a wide variety of professions. They offer a variety of experiences, an excellent source of referance, and permanent placement (in some instances).

School Placement Services

High schools, business schools, trade schools, and colleges have well organized placement services. The placement officer will refer you to positions as well advice you of any problems you may encounter.

```
3583  3591  5153  415  3695  5369  7516  9452  11
3583  3591  5153  415  3695  5369  7516  9452  11
1586  6579  9237  772  2593  3189  6541  1485  58
1586  6579  9237  772  2593  3189  6541  1485  58
```

[0] Zip [4] finger to [0]
[4]
↓
```
4  44  444  1  11  111  0  00  000  014  410  001  40
4  44  444  1  11  111  0  00  000  014  410  001  40
```
[1]
↓
[0]
```
014  410  0258  630  025  890  003  301  108  0117
014  410  0258  630  025  890  003  301  104  3017

01  42  09  93  02  58  94  07  71  01  63  09  92  05
01  42  09  93  02  58  94  07  71  01  63  09  92  05

2058  9503  4712  2593  321  0258  9741  1147  73
2058  9503  4712  2593  321  0258  9741  1147  73
0039  9932  2058  8741  258  5236  9885  2014  65
0039  9932  2058  8741  258  5236  9885  2014  65
```

[.] Zip [6] finger to [.]
[6]
↓
```
6.  3.3  6.6  3.3  3.33  6.66  6.36  63.36  36.63
6.  3.3  6.6  3.3  3.33  6.66  6.36  63.36  36.63
```
[3]
↓
[.]
```
1.1  2.2  3.3  4.4  5.5  6.6  7.7  8.8  9.9  10.00
1.1  2.2  3.3  4.4  5.5  6.6  7.7  8.8  9.9  10.00
```

Phone Numbers
```
316-852-7129
201-783-0288
914-783-3697
516-723-0047

803-641-1867
601-742-3697
919-753-0856
512-752-4173
```

or will list a number you should call. If a post office box if given, the porspective employer does not want people dropping in. The resume gives the employer the opportunity to review your qualifications and background and make and make a selection.

Public Employment Agencies

In 1933 the United states Employment Services was established, and today state employment Agencies are located throughout the United States in convenient locations. You will never have to pay for this service since the agency is subsidized thru taxes.

Private Employment Agencies

Private agencies are excellent source of job openings. Some agencies specialize in certain types of positions while others maybe of a general nature. There is usally a fee involved with may or may not be absorbed by the employers. (Sometimes the fee will be shared.) Although the fee may seem large to you obtaining a position may may be well worth the cost.

Professional Association Agencies

Many professions such as nursing, accountanting, engineering, word processing, etc. maintain employment agencies for members of there respective professions and for college students enter the profession. Check periodicals!

Note   The decimal points should align.

```
$4,123.12
 9,232.47
   902.17
 7,418.92

  712.365
   89.257
  123.009
    7.360
```

Progress Check   It is time to check your progress. At this point you certainly will *not* be typing 200 dpm. However, with practice, your speed will increase.

```
1  4  8  5  26  31  48  852  114  79  635  001          7
3  0  2  8  52  19  93  295  159  37  357  587          14

1      2      3      4      5      6      7
_____


345  679  90l  263  321  147  741  123  121          7
387  741  369  002  258  147  789  963  256          14
203  682  005  510  119  663  228  841  123          21
306  650  258  951  147  474  336  920  147          28
369  521  147  985  220  036  541  752  210          35

1      2      3      4      5      6      7
_____
```

Professional organizations

Many professional organizations post job openings on their web sites. Check out those in your trade or profession.

Want Ads

Check regularly the want ads of your local newspaper to familiarize yourself with the types of jobs that are available and the salaries connected with same. them Remember however that only 20% of the available jobs are listed in the want ads and many may have already been filed.

Be aware of the language used in these want ads and what they really mean.

"fee paid" (who pays it)?
"excellent benefits" (low pay?)
"convenient location" (depending on where you live)
"miscellaneous responsibilities" (looking for a maid?)
"can assume responsibility" (you have to do everything?)
"easy to get along with" (they are or you should be?)
"must have drivers license" (with the price of gas, they may be looking for a chaufer)
chauffeur

Avoid ads that require employees to make a deposit of of money, to purchase sample goods, etc. Such advertisements may merely be ploys to sell goods. Most ads will ask that you submit a resume

```
22 14 78 52 36 95 02 02 22 30 25 55        7
36 02 10 15 36 95 20 14 07 52 02 64        14
52 21 47 96 32 58 56 90 01 13 14 22        21
32 02 58 79 14 21 12 23 36 58 74 40        28
39 99 55 11 47 12 56 30 09 58 74 11        35

1      2      3      4      5      6      7
```

BRAIN BUSTER #7

Beastasaurus Rex

Type the "animal expressions" corresponding to the following.

Example: cowardly = chicken

1. people who stay up late
2. warring
3. pretend to be asleep
4. stubborn
5. not too young
6. have an honest discussion
7. test case
8. final annoyance that pushes one to the limit
9. complex or difficult problem
10. generous supplier

Possible answers are on page 194.

POUNDING THE PAVEMENT

Once you have aquired the necessary skills and have zeroed in on a profession or trade, finding an appropiate placement is your next step. If you can not rely on other people to get you a job—you you must "sell yourself" Many people complain that there are jobs out there. Remember, no one will come nocking at your door; it is you who must take the initiative. Inform freinds, relatives, and former employers of your quest and immediately follow up all leads. Send resumes to local companies in which you are interested check the want adds, register with employment agencies, contact your school placement service, and most important of all—PERSEVERE!

Online job sites

Online job sites are poplar ways to hunt for openings. Check out sites such as www.monster.com, www.jobsonline.net, www.job-hunt.org, and other. Some of of the sites offer tips on resume writing and other useful information.

Social networking sites

Social networking is no longer the domain of teenagers who are posting their diaries. These sites are used for serious business. Check out sites such as www.linkedin.com others in order to find people you've worked with and information about companies you may be interested in.

Words, Words, Words!

The following exercises incorporate a variety of typewriting skills. Type each exercise *exactly* as it appears.

Help Menu   Refer to your Help menu or user manual for the following:

- Left Justify
- Center Justify
- Right Justify
- Accents and Diacritical Marks

EXERCISE 1

Letter Combinations

Vowels and Diphthongs

ai
```
chains daily praise sailing tailgate Saint
unfailing trail mailbags Haiti grains jail
quaint nailbrush maintenance paid rainbows
raise praiseworthy prairie mainframe faint
gainsay haircut assail aisle caisson aioli
```

ea
```
ear each teachers teaches beach breach leach
beads leader least reach reached reads ready
sea seas meals seals real steam earnest zeal
gear early earnings earth earthly eaves bear
peaceful beaches dead lead earliest earldoms
```

ei
```
heir rein receive conceit either neither
surveillance freight seize leisure reign
height weight neighborhood their receipt
ceiling sleigh counterfeit neigh foreign
perceive deign skein feigned deity ceiba
forfeited seizure seismic meiosis either
```

Exercises 1 and 2 have been proofread and edited by hand. Type each one carefully and correctly.

EXERCISE 1

] DRESSING FOR BUSINESS [(center)

Have you ever walked into an office and have been greeted by a secretary wearing a halter or flimsy blouse and miniskirt? Just think of the image that conjures up. The image is a negative one, reflecting poorly on the secretary and the office. This kind of attire might be appropriate for a secretary working in a hotel in Acapulco, but is it not appropriate for a secretary working in a conventional office. Be aware of separating your professional wardrobe and your leisure wardrobe. What you wear makes a statement about your attitudes, your goals, your moods, and your feelings. If you want to get ahead in the business world, dress appropriately.

(indent)
(sp)
Dress standards vary in different parts of the country. For example, in Calif. and Florida, warm weather climates, people tend to dress more simply and casually than their counterparts in New York and boston, where dress tends to be savvy, accessorized, and chic. In Washington, DC, the center of politics, and in the midwest, dress tends to be more understated. Also, some industries, such as banking, call for conservative clothing. Observe those in your organization that you admire and whose jobs you would like to have, and pattern your habits after those people.

ia	piano pianist biased hiatus Iberian Miami phobias riata Siamese diabolic MIA liable liaisons giants fiasco dialogues diamonds CIA utilitarian editorial material sialic bacteria negotiable financially essential ecclesiastical Niagara diastasis hysteria
ie	ancient glacier quiet proficient species lieu thief view lien piety sienna shield relief wield lief chief friend frontiers client belief relieve handkerchief fiend yield field achieve interview sufficient hygienic fiercely fiendish diesel diesis
oi	oil choice diploid poignant point toilet soiree roister roil moisturizer toilsome loitered loincloth adjoining hoity-toity doily coin coinage coincide coincidental boilerplate boisterous pointless jointed
ou	oust couch boundary count thought fought louder pounce country county counterfeit grouch our yours mountain outfield route tournament tourism southern poultry sour roughness quotation Louis boulevard four fourth doubles grounded joyous household

EXERCISE 2

Consonants

ch	cheer each watch hatch check chore chain chicken teach teacher grouch pouch peach peachy much latch chews chairperson inch cinches rich richer richest chose choose chronic clutch brochure church bronchial cherished enchantment Christian achieves

Proofreaders' Marks Some people still prefer to proofread from paper copy because they can lay out the pages and see the continuity. You can find a complete chart of proofreaders' marks on page 147.

Using Proofreaders' Marks

Rail

Although no single mode of trasnportation will be able to meet the full range of transportation needs, our rail rail system has always been, and continued to be one of the hall marks of our nation's transportation infrastructure.

Corrected Text

RAIL

Although no single mode of transportation will be able to meet the full range of transportation needs, our rail system has always been, and continues to be, one of the hallmarks of our nation's transportation infrastructure.

Timed Typing

When you proofread, you are trying to find all the	10
mistakes. Are there any letters in a word omitted?	20
Are there extra letters in a word? Are any letters	30
transposed? Are words properly capitalized? Is the	40
punctuation correct? Are words transposed? Are all	50
the quotation marks both opened and closed? Is the	60
formatting correct? Did you double-check spellings	70
of names? Are the dates correct? Have you used the	80
spell checker in your software? Did you verify the	90
continuity of numbering schemes, such as pages and	100
numeric listings? Have you paid close attention to	110
homonyms? Remember...quality control is your job.	120

1   2   3   4   5   6   7   8   9   10

Proofreading and Editing   137

ck check sickness thick thicker thickest pickle
quick mackerel chuck back duckweed bickering
acknowledgment pack package o'clock rocketry
Rocky Rockies tackle tacky tackiness cracker
crackling wacky checking hackneys greenstick
fickle dicker duck reckless poppycock ruckus

fl flame flagitious muffled flamboyant flavor
flan inflation flaw flashlight flat-footed
Flemish float fluid flowers deflower flood
fluctuated fluoridate fluster fluorocarbon
fledglings inflexible inflammable inflated
affliction affluence influenced conflation

ght right bright fight flight might mightier
sought ought height unsightly thoughtful
thoughtless sightless righteous frighten
tightrope drought draught lights freight
heightened weight insight frighten tight

nd end and founds stand stranded expandable
fund grind ground lend sender underscore
handiest endlessly condolences standards
recommend pretend land landed contending
landlord London abound compound handling
indent plundered panda expand expandable

nt current event continual meant continents
hint printouts spent pantomime gentleman
mentally intelligently intensive antenna
antagonist entered banter central dental
gentlemen latent pent sentence ventilate
tentatively faintly quaintly paint Saint

Words, Words, Words!

Identify Your Key Issue. If your reader forgets just about everything you write, what's the one key point you want him or her to remember? Distill this key point into one sentence. This step is critical to delivering a clear and targeted message.

One of the characteristics of successful businesspeople is the ability to communicate articulately. The National Center on the Evaluation of Quality in the Workplace lists communications skills as one of the two leading job skills employees must have. (Attitude is the other.) No matter what you write—letters, memos, emails, reports, proposals, presentations, handbooks or anything else—you can write with confidence and competence and actually enjoy the process! Create strategic documents your readers read first, documents that drive action, documents that affect your readers as you wish. Following are eight steps for doing just that:

1. **Understand Your Audience.** You must see your target so you know where to aim. Ask yourself these questions. Then answer them.

- What does my reader *need to know* about the subject?
- What's the benefit to the reader?
- What will my reader's reaction be to the message?

2. **Identify Your Key Issue.** If your reader forgets just about everything you write, what's the one key point you want him or her to remember? Distill this key point into one sentence. This step is critical to delivering a clear and targeted message.

Final Text

One of the characteristics of successful businesspeople is the ability to communicate articulately. The National Center on the Evaluation of Quality in the Workplace lists communications skills as one of the two leading job skills employees must have. (Attitude is the other.) No matter what you write—letters, memos, emails, reports, proposals, presentations, handbooks or anything else—you can write with confidence and competence and actually enjoy the process! Create strategic documents your readers read first, documents that drive action, documents that affect your readers as you wish. Following are eight steps for doing just that:

1. **Understand Your Audience.** You must see your target so you know where to aim. Ask yourself these questions. Then answer them.

- What does my reader *need to know* about the subject?
- What's the benefit to the reader?
- What will my reader's reaction be to the message?

2. **Identify Your Key Issue.** If your reader forgets just about everything you write, what's the one key point you want him or her to remember? Distill this key point into one sentence. This step is critical to delivering a clear and targeted message.

ph

photo photograph photographer photography physicians physiological physical physics physique phonetic unphotogenic phonograph phase pharmacy phalanx graph sophisticate phi sophomore aphid aphrodisiac Aphrodite ophthalmological hermaphrodite phenomenon

qu

quota quite quit quiet equals equated aqua equality equip equity aqua quote quotation quarry quarreled qualify quartz quadrupled unqualified unique quarter quarterly Queen quest quaked earthquake quickening banquet quick quicker quickest acquaint aquamarine

sh

should wish mash shovel show showroom shell shopping shimmer pushover publishing relish mushroom leash kinship Washington refreshes shrine devilish shellac shame shield upshot foreshadows rushing inshore bashful ashamed wishy-washy sheltered sheathe shebang sharp

st

stop stay steer yeast first last least longest student stubborn thirsty worst straight strike statistical persistent moist industrial history honest feasts forecast strays dusty customers stormy bookstore astronaut opportunist latest osteopath stereotype stethoscope stern

str

straight stretchers stricken strew stress strangely street structures strove strung strychnine strudel struggle strong stroll strophe stroke stripling stringent string

MODULE 12

Proofreading and Editing

```
Eye here you.
Eye sea you.
Eye no ewe.
```

Check each document carefully for spelling, formatting, styling, English usage, word repetition, omissions, spacing, transpositions, names and addresses, numbers, and the general sense of the text.

Proofread Carefully

Don't turn on your computer and turn off your brain. Although grammar checkers and spell checkers work well, they're no substitute for the human eye. For example, spell checkers don't know the difference between *see* and *sea* or *no* and *know*, as you see above.

Track Changes

Word processing software comes with a feature that lets you keep a record of your edits. In Microsoft Word, this feature is called Track Changes and is found under Tools. You can send an original document to someone and that person can use Track Changes to edit online. The changes will appear in a different color from the original. Below you see original text, edited text, and final text, which you see when you turn off Track Changes.

Original Text

What do successful businesspeople have in common? The ability to articulately communicate. The National Center on the Evaluation of Quality in the Workplace lists communications skills as one of the two leading job skills employees must. No matter what you write—letters, memos, e-mail messages, reports, proposals, presentations, handbooks or anything else—you can write with confidence and competence and actually enjoy the process! Create strategic documents your readers read first, documents that drive action, documents that affect your readers as you wish. Following are eight steps for doing just that:

Understand Your Audience. You must see your target so you know where to aim. Ask yourself these questions. Then answer them.

- What does my reader need to know about the subject?
- What's the benefit to the reader?
- What will my reader's reaction be to the message?

th	the this that those these though thought thank throng they theory thesis southern northern with without health wealth thin thick therefore thunder therapist worthy width youthfully theater thicket thinner throat menthol methodical plethora three
tr	tree trace truth true truism trout trade truly untrue trust trial trail ventricle trivial travels traitor trait triangular sentry intrepid intrastate intrude truck putrid tributary entreaty country putrid trunks atrophied transfusion trichinosis

EXERCISE 3

Complete the Word

Type each word and insert the missing *a* and/or *o*.

v_lume	th_nk	kn_w	s_n
c_nn_t	re_ch	s_ci_l	at_p
f_ll_w	h_ppy	_bout	br__d

Type each word and insert the missing *i* and/or *e*.

beh_nd	d_ta_l	_nch	r_cent
fa_nt	caus_	l_ed	_rase
lin_s	fr__nd	n__ghbor	s_nd

EXERCISE 4

Three-, Four-, and Five-Letter Words

Three-Letter Words

owl vow cab its ask yet oar map far hog axe
lip and but his was met sat fit net lot due
fib kit rat fan got gin quo yes our gym its
ass get inn tax box wow put yap keg lob cab

BRAIN BUSTER #12

Hyperboles, Metaphors, Similes, and Clichés

Type a corresponding figure of speech that is a hyperbole, metaphor, simile, or cliché.

Example: unreal = phony as a $3 bill

1. raining heavily
2. starving
3. gluttonous
4. very elderly
5. extremely busy
6. gab incessantly
7. irate
8. speeding
9. familiar with a location
10. lose a lot of money

Possible answers are on page 196.

Reports and Manuscripts

Four-Letter Words	kept envy join pots next zone quit sell pale
	gave oxen fuel isle calf maid zany quit sell
	them send were next mine your ours them want
	vest quit many oust yarn belt rest over hate

Five-Letter Words	audit panel poets title quite unite haven
	given woven merit chair ivory yearn liver
	zoned world eight forth laugh knife forty
	petty truly earns quest about doubt could

EXERCISE 5

Separate Hands

Left Hand Only	war bet far axe fare beat gave rave freed
	saw few car bar were cave ears rest tease

Right Hand Only	him pop pin hum jump punk plum jolly knoll
	lip pun mop noun moon hymn onion limp milk

EXERCISE 6

Seeing Double

Double Letters	see off doll feel been putt huff happy fully
	all ill took noon buzz room look marry nippy
	inn aah mitt ooze feet ally jazz weeds mommy
	egg odd adds errs teem bull till funny savvy
	freedom loosely dapper little dabbled manner
	beetle Balaam Ossian pizza sniffle storeroom
	heel foolish aardvarks assistance bookkeeper
	coolant engrossing letter pannier toothbrush

EXERCISE 6

Works Consulted • top-bound

Works Consulted

"Aristotle." *The Houghton Mifflin Dictionary of Biography.* Boston: Houghton Mifflin Company, 2003.

Brushaw, Charles T., Gerald J. Alred, and Walter E. Oliu. *Handbook of Technical Writing.* 2d ed. New York: St. Martin's Press, 1982.

Chambers, Robert. *Cyclopaedia of English Literature.* 2 vols. New York: World Publishing House, 1987.

Dyer, Richard, "The New View at Tanglewood." *Boston Globe*, June 10, 1994, p. 49.

Foner, Eric, and John A. Garraty, eds. *The Reader's Companion to American History.* Boston: Houghton Mifflin Company, 1991.

Hart, James D. *The Oxford Companion to American Literature.* 5th ed. New York: Oxford University Press, 1983.

Lindsell-Roberts, Sheryl. *Strategic Business Letters and E-mail.* Boston: Houghton Mifflin Company, 2004.

Smiley, Xan. "Misunderstanding Africa." *Atlantic*, September 1982, pp. 70–79.

Velasquez, Joyce A. "The Format of Formal Reports." Report prepared for the Southern Engineering Company. Johnson City, Miss. May 29, 1985.

EXERCISE 7

Popular Phrases

Common Phrases

thank you/ as soon as/ we shall be happy/
if you have/ have you/ of the/ with us/ from you/
you should/ we are/ after which/ if you can/
this is/ that was/ if you have/ of course/ I hope

Letter Phrases

as you know/ this will confirm/ on behalf of/
as soon as possible/ enclosed you will find/
we would appreciate/ our records show that/
please take this opportunity/ in response to/
self-addressed, stamped envelope

Salutations

Dear Sir or Madam:/ Ladies and Gentlemen:/
Dear Mr. Anthony:/ Dear Mrs. McGulloch:/
To Whom This May Concern:/ To the Staff:

Complimentary Closing

Very truly yours,/ Yours truly,/ Sincerely,/
Sincerely yours,/ Respectfully yours,/ Yours
respectfully,/ Cordially,/ Best wishes,

EXERCISE 8

Foreign Expressions

Use accent marks where appropriate. You will find them in characters for foreign words.
See page 6 for examples.

à la mode/ avant-garde/ bona fide/ bon appétit/
carte blanche/ señora/ maitre d'hôtel/ per
diem/ modus operandi/ jalapeño/ ex post facto/
prima facie/ garçon/ santé/ gracias/ carpe diem

• left-bound

Works Cited

2"

1"   1"

1.   Jennie Mason, *Introduction to Word Processing* (Indianapolis: Bobbs-Merrill, 1981), p. 55.

2.   John E. Warriner and Francis Griffith, *English Grammar and Composition* (New York: Harcourt Brace Jovanovich, 1977), p. 208.

3.   Ruth I. Anderson et al., *The Administrative Secretary: Resource* (New York: McGraw-Hill, 1970), p. 357.

4.   Simone de Beauvoir, *The Second Sex*, trans. and ed. H.M. Parshley (New York: Alfred A Knopf, 1953), p. 600.

5.   Alfred H. Markwardt, *American English*, ed. J.L. Dillard (New York: Oxford University Press, 1980), p. 94.

6.   Martha L. Manheimer, *Style Manual: A Guide for the Preparation of Reports and Dissertations*, Books in Library and Information Science, vol. 5 (New York: Marcel Dekker, 1973), p. 14.

7.   Charles T. Brushaw, Gerald J. Alred, and Walter E. Oliu, *Handbook of Technical Writing*, 2d ed. (New York: St. Martin's Press, 1982), pp. 182–184.

8.   National Micrographics Association, *An Introduction to Micrographics*, rev. ed. (Silver Spring, Md.: National Micrographics Association, 1980), p. 42.

9.   *The World Almanac and Book of Facts* (New York: Newspaper Enterprises Association, Inc., 1985), p. 310.

10.   *Rules for Alphabetical Filing as Standardized by ARMA* (Prairie Village, Kans.: Association of Records Managers and Administrators, 1981), p. 14.

11.   Peggy F. Bradbury, ed., *Transcriber's Guide to Medical Terminology* (New Hyde Park, N.Y.: Medical Examination Publishing Co., 1973), p. 446.

12.   Kemp Malone, "The Phonemes of Current English," *Studies for William A. Read*, ed. Nathaniel M. Caffee and Thomas A. Kirby (Baton Rouge: Louisiana State University Press, 1940), pp. 133–165.

13.   Robert Chambers, *Cyclopaedia of English Literature*, 2 vols. (New York: World Publishing House, 1875), vol. I, p. 45.

EXERCISE 9

Building a Sentence

User Manual
Left Justify

```
Always
Always be
Always be sure
Always be sure to
Always be sure to keep
Always be sure to keep your
Always be sure to keep your eyes
Always be sure to keep your eyes on
Always be sure to keep your eyes on the
Always be sure to keep your eyes on the copy!
```

Center Justify

```
                        It's
                   It's important
                  It's important to
                 It's important to be
               It's important to be computer
            It's important to be computer literate
         It's important to be computer literate now.
```

Right Justify

```
                                                    Be
                                               Be sure
                                            Be sure to
                                      Be sure to check
                                Be sure to check every
                        Be sure to check every homonym
             Be sure to check every homonym carefully.
```

Words, Words, Words!

EXERCISE 4

Body of Report
- left-bound
- two columns
- left justify
- footnote with superscript

Purpose

This study documents the benefits and costs of potential U.S. Coast Guard Vessel Traffic Services (VTS) in selected U.S. deep draft ports on the Atlantic, Gulf, and Pacific coasts. The U.S. Department of Transportation, Research, and Special Programs Administration (RSPA), Volpe National Transportation Systems Center (VNTSC), conducted the study for the U.S. Coast Guard, Office of Navigation Safety and Waterway Services, Special Projects Staff. The study started in February 1990 as a Coast Guard initiative, prior to the passage of "The Oil Pollution Act of 1990"(Public Law 101-380). This initiative satisfies the requirements of the Act.

Background

The concept of VTS has gained international acceptance by governments and maritime industries as a means of advancing safety in rapidly expanding ports and waterways. Vessel Traffic Services work through position and situation advisory communications with vessels navigating the waterways. VTS communications are advisory in nature, providing timely and accurate information to the mariner, thus enhancing the potential for avoiding vessel casualties. VTS does not exercise direct control by ordering specific course directions or speeds to maneuver around hazards. "While the Vessel Control Center (VTC) will have the authority to direct the movement of a vessel in a dangerous situation, a master remains responsible for the safe and prudent maneuvering of the vessel at all times."[1]

Several spills following within three months of the Prince William Sound incident of March 1989 (i.e., one in the coastal waters of Rhode Island, one in the Delaware River, and one in the Houston Ship Channel) drew intense congressional interest and resulted in the passage of "The Oil Pollution Act of 1990" (Public Law 101-380) on August 18, 1990. The Act requires the "secretary to conduct a study…to determine and prioritize the U.S. ports and channels that are in need of new, expanded, or improved vessel traffic service systems…." The Act further requires that the results of the study be submitted to Congress not later than one year after enactment of the Act.

Several studies have been performed prior to this study:

1. The USCG Study Report *Vessel Traffic Systems: Analysis of Port Needs* (August 1973)
2. The BMC Hong Kong VTS Study,

---

[1] Federal Register, Vol. 55, No. 166, August 27, 1990, Rules and Regulations, pg. 34909

EXERCISE 10

Homonyms and Commonly Confused Words

Type the sentences below and include the missing word from the choices to the left. The correct answers are on page 72.

to, two, too
1. The _____ attorneys had _____ many decisions _____ make.

a lot, allot
2. _____ of people do not _____ their time wisely.

capital, capitol
3. The _____ is located in Boston, the _____ of Massachusetts.

their, they're, there
4. _____ going to establish _____ new business over _____ if permission is granted.

correspondence, correspondents
5. The three _____ sent their _____ via air mail, but it did not arrive for three days.

personnel, personal
6. The _____ department has access to all the company's records. Some are rather _____.

chose, choose
7. I _____ the red dress; you should _____ the blue one.

who's, whose
8. _____ going to take _____ place in the race tomorrow?

its, it's
9. _____ the right time for the corporation to make _____ decision.

principal, principle
10. The _____ is a woman of very high _____s.

stationery, stationary
11. The _____ tables could not be removed for the _____ to be displayed.

Words, Words, Words!

The following are some basic colors and the emotions or responses they invoke.

COLOR	EMOTION/RESPONSE
Pink	Gets a message across and subdues anger. (Why do you think they call it a "pink slip"?)
Yellow	Optimistic and cheery—will get an audience's attention.
Dark Blue	Puts everyone in a soothing and tranquil mood.
Pale Blue	Good in the summer because it can make people feel the room is actually 3–4 degrees cooler than it actually is.
Red	Demands attention and makes people alert.
Green	Shows speed.

Design Criteria

When you are preparing any visual, keep in mind visibility, clarity, and simplicity. All visuals should have a uniform look. Use uppercase and lowercase for the text; it will be easier to read than all capital letters. The headings can be in all capital letters.

2

quite, quiet

12. They were _____ at home in the _____ neighborhood.

except, accept

13. I will _____ the offer, _____ for the deadline. We need more time.

past, passed

14. In the _____, I _____ your house on the way from work.

than, then

15. The brown house costs more _____ the blue; _____ comes the brown.

already, all ready

16. I _____ told you that we will be _____ no later than nine.

all together, altogether

17. The family was _____ for the reading of the will, but no one was _____ pleased with its contents.

all right, alright

18. Will it be _____ to make the delivery tomorrow?

sight, site

19. The _____ of the new building is a scenic _____.

later, latter

20. Of the two books, the _____ is the _____ edition.

advise, advice

21. I _____ you not to give out free _____.

no, know

22. I _____ there is _____ chance that he is correct.

altar, alter

23. After the bride and groom meet at the _____ it will be a little too late to _____ their relationship.

EXERCISE 3

Body of Report

- top-bound
- double-spaced
- page numbers should be centered at the bottom of the page

GENERAL PRINCIPLES FOR PREPARING VISUALS

The purpose of a visual is to reinforce and clarify an idea; it should not contain anyone's verbatim presentation. Equate a slide or viewgraph with an article in a magazine. The picture in a magazine is the highlight that is supported by the text. Highlight slides and viewgraphs reinforce and drive home the speaker's main points. Use visuals effectively to

- open a presentation
- channel thinking
- emphasize key points
- represent numerical or financial information
- show comparisons
- simplify a process
- explain a new concept

Do not plan too many visuals for a single presentation. Only the high points need to be illustrated, not every thought.

Understanding the Effects of Color

Color has been shown to have an emotional appeal to which people respond. It is recommended that slides be prepared on a dark background with lighter printing and that viewgraphs be prepared on a lightly tinted background with dark printing.

1

Reports and Manuscripts

assistance, assistants	24. His three _____ were of great _____ during his long illness.
beside, besides	25. _____ the chair, the basket is _____ the desk.
board, bored	26. The _____ of directors was _____ with the agenda.
done, dun	27. Please do not _____ me any further. As soon as the audit is _____ I will remit my check.
illicit, elicit	28. The con man was trying to _____ money for his _____ project.
adverse, averse	29. _____ weather conditions make me _____ to driving.
formally, formerly	30. They were all dressed _____ for the dance and met all those students who were _____ classmates.
maybe, may be	31. I _____ out of town tomorrow. So _____ you should call before you stop by.
trial, trail	32. The _____ proved that the defendant left a _____ a mile long.
raise, raze	33. The company was willing to _____ the building but would not _____ salaries.
ad, add	34. Please _____ the _____ to your scrapbook.
compliment, complement	35. A full _____ of colors arrived, and I must _____ you on your efforts in bringing it about.

LIST OF FIGURES

1. two, too, to
2. A lot, allot
3. capitol, capital
4. They're, their, there
5. correspondents, correspondence
6. personnel, personal
7. chose, choose
8. Who's, whose
9. It's, its
10. principal, principle
11. stationary, stationery
12. quite, quiet
13. accept, except
14. past, passed
15. than, then
16. already, all ready
17. all together, altogether
18. all right (*alright* isn't a word)
19. site, sight
20. latter, later
21. advise, advice
22. know, no
23. altar, alter
24. assistants, assistance
25. Besides, beside
26. board, bored
27. dun, done
28. elicit, illicit
29. adverse, averse
30. formally, formerly
31. may be, maybe
32. trial, trail
33. raze, raise
34. add, ad
35. complement, compliment

BRAIN BUSTER #8 — *Foodaholic*

Type the "food expressions" corresponding to the following.

Example: cramped = packed in like sardines

1. crazy
2. stuck
3. lousy car
4. flatter
5. very tall and very slim
6. something hunky-dory
7. pokey
8. easy
9. that's the way it is
10. redhead

Possible answers are on page 194.

MODULE 8

Prefixes and Suffixes

Prefixes

Note

Most prefixes are joined to a root word without a hyphen unless the second element begins with a capital letter, e.g., *anti-American*. An exception is the prefix *self-*, which is joined to the second element with a hyphen in all but a few instances, e.g., *selfdom*, *selfhood*. The prefix *re-* is normally joined to a root word without a hyphen unless a distinction must be made between words having more than one meaning, e.g., *recreation*, "sport, play," and *re-creation*, "a new creation."

Type each of the following words.

ante-

antebellum antecede antechamber antedate
antediluvian antefix antemeridian antemortem
antenatal antepenultimate anterior anteroom

anti-

anti-American antiaircraft antibody anticlimactic
antidote antifreeze antigen antigravity antipasto
antipathy antipersonnel antipoverty antisocial
antithesis antitoxin antiviral antiwar

bi-

biannual biathlon biaxial bicarbonate bicentenary
bicentennial bicycle biennial bifocals biform
bigamist bilateral bilingual bimonthly binary
binocular binomial bisect bisexual biweekly

bio-

biochemical biochemistry biodegradable
biodynamics biogenesis biographer biography
biology biomass biomedical bionics biophysics

circum-

circumcise circumduction circumference circumflex
circumlocution circumlunar circumnavigate
circumpolar circumscribe circumscription
circumsolar circumspect circumstantial circumvent

EXERCISE 2

Table of Contents from Technical Report

- left-bound
- set tab for leaders and right justify

com-	comfort commence comment commerce commingle commissioner commit common commune communicate communism compare comparison compassion compatible compel complect complete complex complicate complicity compliment complimentary component compose compound comprehend comprehensible comprehension compress compulsive
con-	concern concert conclude concrete condominium conduce conduct confer conference confide confident confine confinement confiscate conflict conflicting congeal conjugate conjunct consider consideration console consolidate construct converge conversation converse convict convince
dis-	disappoint disarm disarrange disband discharge discipline discuss disfavor disfranchise dishonor disinherit disinterested dislocate disloyal dismember dismiss disorganize disperse dispose disposition dispute disrespectful disrobe
em-	embankment embark embarrass embathe embed embellish embezzle embitter embodiment embody embryo empanada empathy emperor employ employee
en-	enable enact enamor encapsulate enchant enclosure encompass encyclical encyclopedia endanger endorsement endow energy engagement engrave enhance enlist enrage enroll entangle enthuse enthusiastic envelope envoy enwind enwrap
for-	forbearance forever forfeit forget forgiveness forgo forjudge forlorn formerly formidable forsake forsooth forswear forward forwarn

EXERCISE 1

Cover Page
- top- and bottom-centered
- center justify

```
         AN EXPERIMENTAL STUDY TO DETERMINE THE
              EFFECT OF THE SPELLING TEST ON
             THE ABILITY OF STUDENTS TO SPELL


                       Presented to
                     the Faculty of the
               Department of Business Education
               and Office Systems Administration
                  Montclair State College


                           by
                      Sheryl Lorenz
              B.S., Saint Thomas Aquinas College


                      December 20—
```

fore-	forearm forecast foredeck foredoom forego foregoing forehand forehead foreknowing foreleg foreman foremost forenamed forenoon foreordain foreperson forerunner foresight forestall foretell forewarn forewoman foreword
hyper-	hyperacid hyperactive hyperbole hyperbolic hyperboloid Hyperborean hypercharge hypercorrect hypercritical hyperinflation hypermarket hypermedia hypermetric hyperon hyperopia hypersensitive hypersonic hypertension hyperthyroid hypertonic hyperventilation
hypo-	hypoacidic hypoallergenic hypocenter hypochondria hypocrisy hypocritical hypodermic hypodermis hypogene hypoglycemia hyposensitive hypostasis hypothalamus hypothermia hypothesis hypothesize hypothetical hypothyroidism hypoventilation
inter-	interactive interbank intercede interchange intercity intercollegiate intercontinental interdepartmental interfaith intergalactic interlace interlibrary interlock intermingle intermission intermural internalize international internist interoffice interplanetary interpret interrelated interrogate intersect intersection
intra-	intracellular intracoastal intradermal intragalactic intramolecular intramural intramuscular intraocular intrapersonal intraspecific intrastate intravascular
intro-	introduce introduction introductory introjection introspection introspective introversion

---

Styling for Technical Papers or Government Reports

Technical papers and government reports adhere to the guidelines of formal reports; however, they are generally quite rigid in format. There is often a unique numbering scheme that identifies each heading and subdivision.

Numbering Headings and Subdivisions

```
1.0 MAIN HEADING

    1.1 FIRST SUBDIVISION
    1.2 SECOND SUBDIVISION

        1.2.1 Next Level Subdivision
        1.2.2 Next Level Subdivision

            1.2.2.1 Next Level Subdivision
            1.2.2.2 Next Level Subdivision
```

Contents of Technical Papers or Government Reports

Reports of this nature will contain any or all of the following: a cover, title page, preface, table of contents (including a list or lists of figures and tables), executive summary, list of acronyms, appendixes, references, and index.

The following exercises are from a variety of reports and manuscripts. Type each one and refer to the styling mentioned earlier in this Module.

Note

If you are using a font that is not a 12-point monospace, your report will not match this one line for line.

ir-	irradiate irrational irreconcilable irrecoverable irredeemable irreformable irrefutable irrefutably irregular irregularity irrelevant irremovable irreplaceable irrepressible irresistible irresponsible irreverence irrevocable
mis-	misapply misbelief miscall misconduct miscue misdirection misfeasance misfire misfit misgiving misguided misinform misjudge mislead mismanage misnomer misplace misprint mispronounce misrepresent misshapen mistake mistaken mistreat mistrial mistrust misunderstand misuse misword
non-	nonabrasive nonaligned nonattached nonbeliever nonchallenging noncolor noncombatant nonconformity noncritical nondenominational nondurable non-Euclidean nonfactual nonfiction nonglare nonjudgmental nonprofit nonresident nonresistant nonreturnable nonstrategic nontaxable non-U nonunion nonverbal nonviolent
over-	overact overage overburden overcompensation overdrive overdue overhead overinflate overnight overpopulate overrun overseas oversee oversimplify oversleep overstock oversupply overtax overthrow overtime overturn overview
per-	perceive perception perfect performance perfume perfunctory perish perjure perjury perpetrate perpetual perpetuate perpetuity perquisite
pre-	preamble prearrange preaxial prebuilt precaution precede preceding precipitate preclude preconceived precook predate predict predispose preempt prefab preflight prehistoric prelaw preliminary premarital premed prepay prevent

Quotations	**1.** If a quotation is contained within the paragraph, place quotation marks around the quoted material.
	2. If a quotation appears as a separate block, it can be used without quotation marks. The quoted material should be indented from the left and right margins and should be single-spaced.
Pagination	The first page of a report (or chapter of a report) is usually not numbered, although it is considered to be page 1. Your software can suppress the number on the first page.
Footnotes and Endnotes or Works Cited	Whenever you are citing work from another source (whether it is a fact, an opinion, or a quote), you must reference the source. Footnotes, which are no longer popular, are included at the bottom of the page on which the text is cited. Endnotes, also referred to as *Works Cited*, are listed at the end of the manuscript. All cited entries should be numbered and appear in numerical order.
Bibliographies or Works Consulted	Bibliographies are commonly referred to as *Works Consulted*. This would include any material that was used as a reference. All entries should be in alphabetical order by the author's last name.

Timed Typing

```
Itineraries help a traveler keep track of all his/    10
her appointments. When making travel arrangements,    20
it would be helpful to contact a travel agent. The    30
travel agent can help plan the itinerary, make the    40
arrangements, and supply necessary information. If    50
you don't know of a travel agent, contact American    60
Society of Travel Agents. Its address is 666 Fifth    70
Avenue, 12th Floor, New York, NY 10103. The travel    80
agent will need information such as name, dates of    90
departure and arrival, mode of transportation, and   100
all the details of your trip. If you have a hectic   110
schedule, why not let someone else do the legwork!   120
```

```
 1     2     3     4     5     6     7     8     9     10
```

pro-

proactive proceed proceedings proclaim produce
production profane profess professional profit
profound profuse program programmer prologue
pronoun pronounce prophetic proportion prorate
proscribe proscription prosecution protract

re-

react rebuild recede receive reception recital
reclamation recollect re-collect recreation
re-creation recreational reenter refill refine
reform rehabilitate rehearse reimburse
relapse relaxation relay release relief relieve
remedial reproach reputation repute research
residence residuary resign re-sign resigned resume

self-

self-addressed self-assured self-centered
self-contained self-control self-educated
self-employed self-evident self-governing
self-importance self-indulgence self-mailing
self-protection self-reliant self-righteous
self-rule self-styled self-supporting
self-sustaining self-taught self-worth

sub-

subcabinet subcenter subcommittee subdebutante
subdirectory subdue subflooring subhuman subject
sublease submarine submerge suborbital
subordinate subplot subpoena subscript subsoil
substantial substitute subtract suburban subway

super-

superficial superfine superfluous supergalaxy
superimpose superintendent superior superiority
superjet superlative superman supermarket
supernatural supernova supersaturate superscript
superscription supersede superstore supervise

Basic Mansuscript Format

2"

MAIN HEADING
IN
ALL CAPS

left margin 1½"

(½" allowance for binding)

Subheading
Uppercase and Lowercase

Side Heading—Uppercase and Lowercase/Underscored

five-space indentation for paragraphs

double-spaced body

Paragraph Heading—Underscored/Followed by Period.

bottom margin 1"–1½"

1"

2

trans-	transact transcontinental transfer transfigure transformer transgression transient transilluminate transistor translate transliterate translucent transmission transmit transoceanic transparent transpire transplant
un-	unbearable unconscious unconstitutional uncontrollable uncountable undo undue unemployed uneventful unfortunate unnecessary
under-	underage underbid undercoat undercurrent undercut underdog underfoot undergo undergraduate underground underline underpaid underpass underrate undersecretary undersell undershirt undersized underskirt understaff underwrite

Suffixes

-able	changeable comfortable laughable mailable preventable remarkable unquestionable unthinkable
-age	bandage bondage breakage brokerage coinage cordage dosage drainage lineage mileage parentage passage portage postage roughage steerage storage tillage tonnage usage verbiage vicarage wreckage
-al	acquittal additional arrival betrayal central classical conventional denial egotistical fatal fiscal general literal logical magical mechanical medical neutral parental proposal rebuttal recital refusal retrieval rival several signal
-ance	absorptance acceptance clearance continuance elegance endurance grievance ignorance importance performance remembrance significance

Reports and Manuscripts

Written reports are a prime method of obtaining and communicating information. Reports are often written in the third person and deal with facts. A report can take the form of an outline, memorandum, formal report, or graphic illustration.

Help Menu

Refer to your Help menu or user manual for the following:

- Outlines
- Table of Contents
- Margins
- Page Breaks
- Single and Double Spacing
- Pagination
- Charts and Tables
- Bulleted or Numbered Lists
- Superscripts
- Tabs (with leaders)
- Headers and Footers
- Footnotes and Endnotes or Works Cited
- Indexes

Styling for Formal Reports

Headings

Place the main heading and chapter headings 2" from the top of the page. (They are generally centered.)

Margins

1. When the report is to be top-bound, use 1" side margins, $1\frac{1}{2}$" top margins, and 1" bottom margins. The first page should have a 2" top margin.
2. When the report is to be left-bound, use $1\frac{1}{2}$" side margins and 1" top margins.
3. When the report is to be unbound (stapled in the upper left corner), use 1" margins all around.

Paragraphs

You can indent paragraphs 5–7 spaces from the left margin. Some writers do not indent the first paragraph that follows a major heading. This is either company style or individual preference.

-ary	auxiliary boundary centenary contrary dictionary elementary evolutionary honorary imaginary infirmary library literary revolutionary secondary secretary stationary tertiary tributary vocabulary voluntary
-ence	absence audience coherence consequence deference dependence emergence existence experience impertinence independence occurrence
-ful, -fuls	careful cupful cupfuls eventful graceful grateful handful harmful helpful meaningful mindful mouthful mouthfuls powerful spoonful spoonfuls tablespoonful teaspoonful thoughtful useful
-fully	carefully gracefully hopefully meaningfully mindfully regretfully thoughtfully willfully
-graph	autograph choreograph chronograph cryptograph epigraph lithograph logograph mimeograph monograph petrograph phonograph pictograph radiograph seismograph telegraph
-graphy	autobiography biography cinematography petrography stenography typography
-ible	accessible admissible deductible eligible feasible incorrigible intelligible invincible possible reversible tangible transmissible
-ing	accommodating accounting bookkeeping carrying conforming copying dining directing forcing hanging marketing painting performing puzzling reforming relaxing sitting standing studying vacating vacuuming worrying worshiping yachting

BRAIN BUSTER #11

Type the "nautical expressions" corresponding to the following:

Example: tough it out = weather the storm

1. strictly controls

2. rescue

3. from first to last

4. have resentment

5. Watch out!

6. Maintain the status quo.

7. finished

8. give room

9. avoid

10. between a rock and a hard place

Possible answers are on page 195.

-ion	appreciation companion consideration correction corrosion description diction exploration explosion fashion habitation invasion irritation notation permission recreation separation
-ish	boyish brownish childish Danish diminish fiendish Finnish girlish greenish limpish Polish prudish reddish selfish Spanish Swedish yellowish
-ism	Americanism atheism Communism conservatism criticism favoritism federalism feminism feudalism fundamentalism hedonism industrialism Judaism mannerism modernism plagiarism skepticism Socialism synergism Zionism
-ist	antagonist atheist chauvinist columnist communist exhibitionist hedonist fatalist fundamentalist industrialist novelist isolationist Methodist pianist protagonist realist segregationist
-ize	agonize burglarize characterize hypnotize itemize localize modernize ostracize revolutionize
-less	careless cordless countless fearless fruitless hapless heartless meaningless meatless mindless motionless odorless passionless profitless speechless spineless spotless thoughtless
-logy	anthology anthropology biology cardiology climatology cosmology ethnology genealogy gerontology gynecology histology kinesiology neurology ontology phonology psychology radiology technology terminology zoology

Your Street Address
City, State Zip
Current Date

[Person]
[Company]
[Street Address]
[City, State Zip]

Dear [Person]:

Your advertisement in the BOSTON GLOBE for an
Administrative Assistant is of great interest to me.
As you can see from the enclosed resume, I have spent
the last five years as the Administrative Assistant to
the President of The Rolfe Data Company and currently
supervise two secretaries.

My background includes strong computer skills. I have
worked extensively with Microsoft Word and PowerPoint
and have prepared newsletters and slide presentations.
I also have a working knowledge of Excel and basic
bookkeeping skills. My responsibilities have included
setting up trade shows and conferences, as well as
making travel arrangements.

Please give me the opportunity to meet with you
personally to discuss the contribution I can make to
[specific company]. I will call your office next week
to arrange a mutually convenient time.

Sincerely,

Your Name

Enclosure

-ly	brotherly casually duly easterly fatherly formally formerly happily merrily motherly northerly only professionally readily quickly respectfully shortly sincerely sisterly southerly steadily truly verily westerly
-ment	acknowledgment adornment advancement advertisement appeasement arrangement assignment defacement encouragement endorsement entanglement estrangement figment judgment management pigment placement procurement supplement
-ous	adventurous analogous dangerous desirous famous ferrous grievous hazardous hideous joyous libelous marvelous mischievous momentous mountainous murderous outrageous perilous poisonous religious ravenous riotous slanderous
-ure	disclosure enclosure erasure foreclosure fracture judicature lecture legislature literature manufacture puncture rupture structure torture

- Pages reviewed and corrected
- Final page count

I would welcome your suggestions and comments regarding the above so that I can put together a final proposal for Harry that reflects an accurate account of how productive we are.

Customized Form Letters

Help Menu

Features such as Print Merge or Mail Merge will allow you to prepare form letters and customize them so that each one appears to be an original. Refer to your Help menu or user manual for instructions.

EXERCISE 12

Type the form letter that follows and customize it for each of the three recipients:

(1)   Mr. Robert Littlehale, President
Beth Wolf Employment Services
205 Minolta Street
Malden, MA 02148

(2)   Ms. Betty Gau
The Green Mountain Company
66 Warburton Circle
Salem, MA 01970

(3)   Director of Human Resources
Attleboro Chemical Company, Inc.
456 Main Street
Worcester, MA 01602

*Who's Afraid?*

Phobias are abnormal fears. Type the phobia associated with the following fears.

Example: fear of changes = tropophobia

1. closed spaces

2. open spaces

3. water

4. strangers

5. words

6. blood

7. heights

8. darkness

9. marriage

10. getting peanut butter stuck to the roof of your mouth

The answers are on page 195.

this time, but we predict that there will be vacancies soon because several of our tenants have expressed an interest in larger quarters. We shall try to meet their requirements in our new facility. ¶ In addition to reading our literature, please feel free to call any time or—better yet—pay us a visit. Just call a few days in advance, and we'll be happy to make all the arrangements./Sincerely,/Enclosures

EXERCISE 10

Memorandum

Date/To: Our Staff/From: [your name]/Subject: Magazine Subscriptions/Several months ago I distributed a questionnaire requesting information about the magazines you would like us to order for the office. Based on your responses, we are pleased to inform you that we have subscribed to the following magazines, which I hope will be of value: INC, MODERN OFFICE TECHNOLOGY, and PC MAGAZINE./I would appreciate your comments and future recommendations.

EXERCISE 11

Memorandum

Date/To: Fellow Publications Systems Chiefs/From: Eric L. Lindsell/Re: Reporting for Technical Writing/As you know, Harry Lorenz is in the process of preparing a new method of evaluating each person's activities for the week that can be used for each of our departments. He is looking for meaningful statistics (if that isn't a contradiction in terms . . .) that will reflect the contribution each of us is making. ¶ I am proposing that we include the following as part of our weekly status reports:
- Hours of research, planning, and coordination
- Pages drafted

PART THREE

Practical Applications

MODULE **9**

Charts, Tables, and Columns

Charts and Tables

Charts and tables are useful for presenting columns and rows of tabular information. (Columns run vertically and rows run horizontally.) They are also useful for creating invoices, purchase orders, and other forms.

Columns

Columns are useful for information to be presented in a format of two or more columns.

Help Menu   Refer to your Help menu or user manual for the following:

- Tables
- Rows and Columns
- Columnization
- Tabs
- Leaders (also known as Dot Leaders)
- Borders and Boxes

Two-Page Letter (Any Style You Choose)

Date/Mr. Harold Roberts/H&R Roberts, Inc./267 Dallas Parkway/Cambridge, MA 02142-1093 /Dear Mr. Roberts:/ Debbie Hahn, my associate, suggested that I contact you regarding office space in the Greater Boston area. We are owners and developers of industrial, commercial, and office buildings and would like to be helpful in satisfying your office requirements. ¶ At present we have space available in our Metro Office Complex, which is located between Broadway and Main Street in Cambridge. This affords direct access to Boston and many of the area's academic institutions via the "T" and provides easy access to Logan Airport. We are expecting this building to be ready for occupancy in September of this year. The building will contain some very desirable office suites on the seventh and eighth floors, which have not yet been rented—many with beautiful views of the Charles River. ¶ In Worcester, Massachusetts, which is in the central part of the state, we have just completed the construction of a ten-story office complex that has been described as one of the outstanding office complexes in the Commonwealth of Massachusetts, and we expect the facility in Cambridge to be on a par. ¶ I'm enclosing floor plans of these two buildings. Inasmuch as so much space has already been rented, I encourage you to look at these floor plans as soon as possible if you genuinely think you might be interested in planting your roots in the Greater Boston area. In case you are not familiar with the area, I've enclosed an area-wide map together with business information from the Chamber of Commerce. I'm also enclosing a copy of our company's brochure, which lists the buildings we manage. They are all mostly rented at

Timed Typings

A table arranges information in tabulated rows and   10
columns. Rows run from left to right while columns   20
run from top to bottom. Tables must be prepared in   30
a format that is uncluttered and easy to read. And   40
a table in a formal report should be enclosed in a   50
border and numbered and titled. Whether your table   60
is formal or informal, be sure the material is ac-   70
curate, precise, and captures the material easily.   80

1   2   3   4   5   6   7   8   9   10

If you are bound by a style sheet, check that   10
style sheet for items such as how the column heads   20
are to be capitalized, whether they should be bold   30
or italic, whether they should be right aligned or   40
left aligned or centered. You should be consistent   50
in the style and position of captions, titles, and   60
all other information.   64

1   2   3   4   5   6   7   8   9   10

CHARTS AND TABLES

Type the following exercises as they appear. Remember to align all decimals.

Two Columns

EXERCISE 1

• decimal alignment in second column

Invoice Number	Unit Price
344306	$1,000.00
454654	250.00
540567	790.50
458451	550.00
954611	375.50

bulbs started flashing with ideas for collaterals, one of which is using the icons from the program to represent features of the software. ¶ I am excited about the challenges ahead and look forward to making a major contribution to the marketing communications efforts at Marvin Industries./Yours truly,/

EXERCISE 7

Simplified Style

Date/Mal-Ed Corporation/Attn: Becky Gentry, National Sales Manager/24 Airmont Road/Owasso, OK 74055/We are interested in installing vending machines in the lunchroom instead of having the coffee truck visit our facility. We would like machines that dispense coffee, soda, juice, and light snacks. ¶ Our main concern is the limited amount of space available in our small lunchroom; therefore, we would like to have one of your representatives visit us to discuss the feasibility of such an installation./Sincerely,/

EXERCISE 8

Simplified Style

Date/Ms. Ethel Lorenz/Sharfin Insurance Company/3 Ternure Avenue/San Francisco, CA 94120-7439/Re: Policy No. 7216A/In accordance with our telephone conversation of this afternoon, enclosed is a photocopy of my check No. 232 in the amount of $422.20, which is proof of payment. ¶ I trust that my insurance will be reinstated and that this matter will be straightened out immediately. Thank you./

```
              HOLIDAYS AND CELEBRATIONS

   Holiday                  Date

   New Year's Day           January 1
   Lincoln's Birthday       February 12
   Washington's Birthday    February 22
   St. Patrick's Day        March 17
   Memorial Day             Last Monday in May
   Independence Day         July 4
   Labor Day                First Monday in September
   Columbus Day             October 12
   Veteran's Day            November 11
   Thanksgiving             Fourth Thursday in November
   Christmas                December 25
```

Three Columns

EXERCISE 3

Employee	Social Security Number	Hourly Rate
James Smith	122-45-2454	$25.00
Elizabeth Doe	245-35-5678	15.90
Susan Britton	136-35-7863	7.50
John Green	245-56-3557	11.20
Grace Jones	574-46-5675	6.75
Barbara Adams	075-36-7753	8.75
Zelda Nasip	135-43-6753	8.50

very mixed emotions, therefore, that I am tendering my resignation. ¶ I thoroughly enjoyed being part of your organization for the past five years and greatly value your friendship and all the experiences I've had. My association with you has given me great insight, confidence, and empathy. I hope you will visit me when you are in the Boston area. ¶ Although I am delivering this letter to you personally, I wanted to put in writing how wonderful and memorable these years have been./Fondly,/

EXERCISE 5

Semiblock Style

Date/CERTIFIED MAIL, RETURN RECEIPT REQUESTED/Joseph Wheeler, Esq./324 Broadway/Somerville, MA 02145/Dear Mr. Wheeler:/Re: Lease Agreement/Enclosed please find the original and two copies of the lease agreement you sent me on behalf of your clients, Richard and Patricia Schmidt. As per our telephone conversation of this morning, I have deleted Paragraph 12 dealing with payment of utilities, and my initials appear next to the deleted portion. ¶ As soon as Mr. and Mrs. Schmidt have executed their portions of the lease and have returned my copy, I will forward my check in the amount of $1,500./Very truly yours,/enc.

EXERCISE 6

Semiblock Style

Date/Ms. Arlene Karp, Vice President/Marvin Industries, Inc./7 Appleland Road/Parsippany, NJ 07054/Dear Ms. Karp:/I thank you for the time you spent with me at the interview yesterday and hope that you will give me the chance to put my resourcefulness and enthusiasm to work for you. ¶ While reading through some of the literature you gave me, light

PUBLISHING LIST

TITLE	AUTHOR	DATE
Data Processing	Michula	1999
Public Speaking	Wolverin	2000
Let's Talk Business	Smitherson	2010
Business English	Reed	2009

SIGNS OF THE ZODIAC

SIGN	COMMON NAME	DATES
Aries	Ram	3/21 – 4/19
Taurus	Bull	4/20 – 5/20
Gemini	Twins	5/21 – 6/20
Cancer	Crab	6/21 – 7/22
Leo	Lion	7/23 – 8/22
Virgo	Virgin	8/23 – 9/22
Libra	Balance/Scales	9/23 – 10/22
Scorpio	Scorpion	10/23 – 11/21
Sagittarius	Archer	11/22 – 12/21
Capricorn	Goat	12/22 – 1/19
Aquarius	Water Bearer	1/20 – 2/18
Pisces	Fishes	2/19 – 3/20

for Arizona, please give me a call, because I would like to take you out for lunch for old time's sake./
Sincerely,/

Modified Block Style

Date/Mr. and Mrs. Gary Sullivan/66 Smith Hill Road/
Essex Junction, VT 05452/Dear Mr. and Mrs. Sullivan:/
We would like to take this opportunity to welcome you and your family to Vermont and hope that you will spend many happy years in our area—one of the most beautiful places in the country. We have enclosed one of our calendars, which will introduce you to many of the businesses and recreational facilities in the area. ¶ While you are familiarizing yourselves with the surroundings, please stop by our bank. We extend to our customers the highest allowable interest rates, free checking account facilities, safe-deposit boxes, low interest loans, direct payment of utility bills, and the personalized service of our staff. For your convenience, we are open Mondays through Fridays from 9 AM to 3:30 PM, on Friday evenings from 7 PM to 9 PM, and on Saturday mornings from 9 AM to noon. ¶ The enclosed $25 gift certificate can be used to open your first savings account with us./Sincerely,/Enclosure

Modified Block Style

Date/PERSONAL/Elisabeth Wolf/Wolf Jewelry Exchange/305 Fifth Avenue/Suite 100/New York, NY 10010/Dear Beth:/I have recently been accepted as part of the master's program at Northeastern University starting with the fall term. This will offer me the opportunity to continue my education, as I have been wanting to do for so long, and be closer to my family. It is with

Four Columns

EXERCISE 6

```
            TWO-LETTER POSTAL ABBREVIATIONS

Alabama                 AL    Montana              MT
Alaska                  AK    Nebraska             NE
Arizona                 AZ    Nevada               NV
Arkansas                AR    New Hampshire        NH
California              CA    New Jersey           NJ
Colorado                CO    New Mexico           NM
Connecticut             CT    New York             NY
Delaware                DE    North Carolina       NC
District of Columbia    DC    North Dakota         ND
Florida                 FL    Ohio                 OH
Georgia                 GA    Oklahoma             OK
Guam                    GU    Oregon               OR
Hawaii                  HI    Pennsylvania         PA
Idaho                   ID    Puerto Rico          PR
Illinois                IL    Rhode Island         RI
Indiana                 IN    South Carolina       SC
Iowa                    IA    South Dakota         SD
Kansas                  KS    Tennessee            TN
Kentucky                KY    Texas                TX
Louisiana               LA    Utah                 UT
Maine                   ME    Vermont              VT
Maryland                MD    Virginia             VA
Massachusetts           MA    Virgin Islands       VI
Michigan                MI    Washington           WA
Minnesota               MN    West Virginia        WV
Mississippi             MS    Wisconsin            WI
Missouri                MO    Wyoming              WY
```

Type the following letters using the letter style indicated and prepare an envelope for each. Be certain that placement is correct and that each letter is centered both vertically and horizontally. Use the current date and sign your name to each letter. The slash (/) indicates the start of a new line, and the paragraph marker (¶) indicates the start of a new paragraph.

EXERCISE 1

Full Block Style

Date/Marc Alan & Associates/24 Besen Parkway/Box 5100/ New York, New York 10150-5100/Dear Mr. Alan:/Please consider me for the entry-level architect position you are advertising in the Sunday edition of THE NEW YORK TIMES. ¶ As you can see from the enclosed resume, I recently graduated from Massachusetts Institute of Technology with a 3.8 average and spent two years working part-time as a draftsman. I spent summers during high school working as an electrician getting hands-on experience in the building field. Also, I am well versed in CAD/CAM and many other computer applications. While attending college, I was president of Sigma Chi fraternity and was an active member of the debating team and computer club. ¶ Please give me the opportunity to discuss my background at a personal interview. You can reach me at (212) 745-1235./Very truly yours,/Enclosure

EXERCISE 2

Full Block Style

Date/Mr. Marvin Karp/7 Appleland Road/Chicago, IL 60602/Dear Marv:/It is with great pleasure that I read of your much-deserved promotion to Sales Manager of the Southwest region. This honor couldn't have been bestowed upon a more enthusiastic, hard-working, and deserving person. ¶ All of us here in Chicago will miss you but will continue to employ the high ideals and standards you've set. ¶ Before you leave

With Leaders

*• right justify
second column
and use leaders*

```
                    MILESTONES

Approval of concepts. . . . . . . . . . . . . . . . .I
Availability of resources . . . . . . . . . . . . II
Effective operating procedures for
   evaluating benefits . . . . . . . . . . . . . . III
Postdeployment ABC operational
   assessment by manager . . . . . . . . . . . . IV
Planning for existing assessment. . . . . . . . . .V
```

EXERCISE 8

The following is a list of commonly misspelled cities. Supply the appropriate postal abbreviation. (The answers are on page 96.)

```
                  COMMONLY MISSPELLED CITIES

Akron           OH        Memphis              TN
Albuquerque               Miami
Baton Rouge               Milwaukee
Beaumont                  Minneapolis
Berkeley                  New Orleans
Bridgeport                Omaha
Buffalo                   Philadelphia
Chattanooga               Phoenix
Chicago                   Pittsburgh
Cincinnati                Racine
Cleveland                 Raleigh
Des Moines                San Francisco
Detroit                   Savannah
Duluth                    Seattle
Gary                      Shreveport
Honolulu                  Syracuse
Knoxville                 Tucson
Lincoln                   Wilkes-Barre
Louisville                Wilmington
Macon                     Worcester
```

Charts, Tables, and Columns

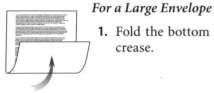

Folding and Inserting a Letter

For a Large Envelope

1. Fold the bottom face up, slightly less than one third of the length, and make a crease.

2. Fold the top third down and make a crease. This will enable the reader to view the letterhead before reading the contents of the letter.

3. Insert the letter with the last crease directed toward the bottom of the envelope.

For a Small Envelope

1. Fold the bottom face up, slightly less than a half inch from the top.

2. Fold the right side one third to the left.

3. Fold the remaining third to the right and make a crease.

4. Insert the letter with the last crease directed toward the bottom of the envelope.

EXERCISE 9

• *right justify*
Arabic numerals
• *left justify*
Roman numerals

ROMAN NUMERALS

1	I	30	XXX
2	II	35	XXXV
3	III	40	XL
4	IV	50	L
5	V	60	LX
6	VI	70	LXX
7	VII	80	LXXX
8	VIII	90	XC
9	IX	100	C
10	X	200	CC
11	XI	300	CCC
12	XII	400	CD
13	XIII	500	D
14	XIV	600	DC
15	XV	700	DCC
16	XVI	800	DCCC
17	XVII	900	CM
18	XVIII	1000	M
19	XIX	1500	MD
20	XX	1800	MDCCC
21	XXI	1890	MDCCCXC
22	XXII	1920	MCMXX
23	XXIII	1950	MCML
24	XXIV	1959	MCMLIX
25	XXV	2000	MM

Preparing the Envelope

The post office uses optical character readers (OCRs) in many large cities to expedite mail processing and delivery and requests adherence to the following guidelines in order to increase the speed and accuracy of mail delivery:

- Type the address in all capital letters and don't use punctuation marks.
- If there isn't a preprinted return address, type your name and return address in the upper left corner.
- If there is an attention line in your mailing address, place it on the first line, above the company name.
- Use capitalized abbreviations for directions (N, E, NE), streets (ST, AVE, RD, BLVD), suites or units (STE, APT, RM), etc.
- Type the Zip Code on the last line of the address, two spaces or three spaces to the right of the two-letter state abbreviation.

```
DONNA RANDALL
61 ENDICOTT ST                  2"
SALEM MA 01970-1234



                                DR ERIC LINDSELL
                                CHIROPRACTICS INC
                4"              5604 FRESH AIRE RD
                                COLUMBIA MD 21044-5076
```

LARGE (No. 10) ENVELOPE

Table Within a Report

EXERCISE 10

Type the full text of this two-page report.

Business Successes
- Has value on an individual basis and on a component basis during the cycle.
- Speeds up the user requirements analysis and yields better results than traditional approaches.
- Involves compressing the normal interviewing sessions into intensive group-participation workshops.

Advantages
- Results are comprehensive because all the concerned people are involved.
- It achieves buy-off for a given project because everyone is made aware of the information needed.
- The group comes to a consensus regarding the necessary functionality and the priorities of these functions. This is especially helpful in the qualifying and scoping process.

Participants
- Workshop leader
- Users of the proposed system
- Business personnel familiar with the current processes
- Technical personnel familiar with the existing or proposed new systems
- Scribe

Memorandum   Type this memorandum as it appears. Supply the current date and type your initials instead of *xx*. A memo does not have to be vertically centered and the heading may vary.

```
Date:     Current

To:       All Office Personnel

From:     Brooke Lindsell

Subject:  Proper Memo Style


The main purpose of a memo is to transmit ideas,
decisions, suggestions, etc., to other members of
an organization. If the organization uses memos
frequently, it will generally have printed memo
forms.

The heading should contain the four elements you see
above, but the placement can vary slightly.

On a memo the inside address, salutation, and
complimentary closing are eliminated. The body starts
three lines below the heading.

xx
```

KEY PEOPLE	ROLE/SKILLS NEEDED
Leader	• Run the meetings. • Keep the group on track. • Have excellent communication skills. • Feel very comfortable working in front of a group.
Scribe	• Record the proceedings of the meetings. • Take care to divide the proceedings into the following categories: data models, information usages, perceived problem areas, solutions and incentives, unresolved (open) issues, unanswered questions.

COLUMNS

First, type "So You Want to Be a Writer!" as a single-column report, using left justification. Second, convert the report you typed into two columns. Third, convert the report into three columns. See an example of the two- and three-column conversion following the single-column format.

Note

If you are using a font that is not a 12-point monospace, your report will not match this one on a line-by-line basis.

Mr. and Mrs. Harold Roberts
Page 2
Date

5. The second page of a two-page letter should be on plain bond paper, not letterhead. Start the page with the name of the addressee, a Page 2 notation, and the date.

6. The second page of the letter should not be vertically centered. It should include at least two lines of text.

I have enclosed a pamphlet on letter writing that you should find useful. If I can be of further help, don't hesitate to contact me.

Sincerely,

Jon A. Roberts

xx
Enclosure

SO YOU WANT TO BE A WRITER!

Everyone has a story to tell or valuable information they'd like to share. Some manuscripts get published and others merely collect dust on the author's bookshelf. Not everyone becomes a household legend like Agatha Christie or James Michener, let alone William Shakespeare, but there is hope for us—for the unknowns. After all, every famous author was once an unknown.

If you want to write a book and are serious about getting it published, you must be armed with a computer, a current edition of WRITER'S MARKET (which is updated annually), and thick skin. I include *thick skin* because the stream of rejections can be devastating. One thing you must remember: A publisher is never rejecting you personally. Writing is subjective, so what may not appeal to one editor in a company may appeal to another. Also, many publishers prepare a five-year publishing plan, and your manuscript might not fit into that plan. (That's a typical rejection excuse.)

MY HUMBLE BEGINNINGS
I never aspired to be a writer; my writing career was spawned quite by accident. I was teaching paralegal skills for a small postsecondary business school. One day, the secretary left me a note saying that a woman from a major dictionary publisher had called and was looking for someone to rewrite a dictionary. Since I'd never worked on dictionaries, I folded the note and (for some unknown reason) tossed it in my pocketbook. Several weeks later the note fell on the floor,

Type this two-page full block letter as it appears. Supply the current date and type your initials instead of *xx*. Be certain that placement of the parts of the letter is correct and that the letter is vertically and horizontally centered on the first page and horizontally centered on the second page.

Date

Mr. and Mrs. Harold Roberts
213 Hollywood Avenue
Dallas, TX 75208

Dear Harold and Lorraine:

In response to your letter of October 12, I am providing answers to the questions you posed:

1. The salutation "Dear Sir:" is no longer appropriate when you don't know if the reader is a man or a woman. I would recommend that you use "Dear Sir or Madam:" instead.

2. The subject line is considered part of the letter, not part of the heading. Therefore, it should always be placed two spaces below the salutation. The purpose of the subject line is to direct the reader's attention to the theme of the letter.

3. If additional material will accompany the letter, an enclosure notation should appear at the bottom. This calls the reader's attention to the fact that something besides the letter should be in the envelope.

4. When a copy of the letter is being sent to a third party, a *cc* (carbon copy) notation is typed directly below the enclosure notation. Today, very few, if any, companies are using actual carbon copies, so the letters *pc* (for "photocopy") sometimes appear in place of *cc*.

---

and I thought, "Um, perhaps this is an omen. Let me call this woman Colleen and see what it's all about." (I had always gotten A's on my "What I Did on My Summer Vacation" reports. And I had just been to a Chinese restaurant, and my fortune cookie read, "You will soon change your line of work.") To make a long story short, I got the assignment to write a major chapter for a legal secretarial handbook.

Thereafter, I just knew that the world was waiting for my pearly words! So I put together the beginnings of a manuscript for a book about women returning to the job market. This was back in the 1960s when the idea was relatively new and women were looking for direction and encouragement. I checked what was then the current edition of WRITER'S MARKET (more about that later) and located all the publishers in that genre. I simultaneously submitted the manuscript to several publishers and had nightly dreams of the bidding wars in which they would all be vying to win me over. Well, was I in for a rude awakening. I was rejected by an honor roll of prestigious as well as unknown publishers and could have wallpapered the entire Taj Mahal with their letters. As a matter of fact, I had gotten so used to rejections, I was expecting one from my mother. What kept me going was remembering that Margaret Mitchell's timeless novel, GONE WITH THE WIND, was rejected endlessly along with a host of other well-known classics.

I had spent what was equivalent to the national debt on postage but didn't give up. Finally, two long, grueling years later, I got a positive response from one publisher. It was not the response I had expected, but it was positive

Simplified Style   Type this simplified letter as it appears. Supply the current date and type your initials instead of *xx*. Be certain that placement of the parts of the letter is correct and that the letter is vertically and horizontally centered.

```
Date

Ms. Nicole Robin
36 Setter Way
Minneapolis, MN 55042

SIMPLIFIED STYLE

You no longer have to be concerned with selecting
the appropriate salutation or complimentary closing.
This streamlined letter style is recommended by the
Administrative Management Society and has completely
done away with those troublesome letter openings and
closings.

The subject line (with no notation) appears in
capital letters three lines below the inside address,
and the body appears three lines below the subject
line. The writer's name is typed four lines below
the body and is also in capital letters. Note that
everything is flush with the left margin.

Although this letter style is not commonly used, it
is expected to become more popular in the future
because it is less time-consuming to prepare, thereby
less costly.



JON A. ROBERTS

xx
```

nonetheless. An editor from a New York publishing house had read my manuscript and liked my style of writing. Although that publisher didn't publish the manuscript, I was offered a contract for a book that was compatible with my background. That book has just gone into its third edition, and I have had others published. My determination did pay off.

By the way, my original manuscript on women returning to the job market is still collecting dust on my bookshelf. By now the subject matter is passé and the pages are yellow.

GETTING STARTED

I caution against writing a book in its entirety unless you have a publisher. If you don't find a publisher, you've expended a lot of questionable effort. Instead, write a complete chapter and prepare a fully annotated outline. In most cases, that's all a publisher will require for review purposes. (The manuscript should be double-spaced, single-sided, with 1" margins all around.)

WRITER'S MARKET—an author's bible—will give you all the information you need to submit your manuscript: how to write a query letter, the editor-in-chief of each publishing house, each publisher's specialty, royalty arrangements, and much more. Always include a self-addressed stamped envelope so your manuscript can be returned. (And don't worry about copyrighting your work. No reputable publisher will print your material without your permission.) Expect to wear out the soles of your shoes trekking to the mailbox each day waiting for responses. And then, after your frustration level has tipped the Richter scale and you've given up all hope of seeing your name in print, you get that one, wonderful *yes*.

Semiblock Style   Type this semiblock letter as it appears. Supply the current date and type your initials instead of *xx*. Be certain that placement of the parts of the letter is correct and that the letter is vertically and horizontally centered.

```
                              Date


        Ms. Jacqueline Kim
        36 Lincoln Road
        Monroe, NY 10950

        Dear Ms. Kim:

             Re: Semiblock Style

             The distinguishing features of this letter
        style are that the subject line is indented below the
        salutation and all paragraphs are indented five to
        seven spaces from the left margin.

             It is important to remember that two tabs must
        be used: one for the date and the complimentary
        closing and one for the indentation of the subject
        line and paragraphs.

             If you are in a situation where maximum
        productivity is not essential, this may be your
        preferred style.

                              Sincerely,


                              Jon A. Roberts


        xx
```

SO YOU WANT TO BE A WRITER!

Everyone has a story to tell or valuable information they'd like to share. Some manuscripts get published and others merely collect dust on the author's bookshelf. Not everyone becomes a household legend like Agatha Christie or James Michener, let alone William Shakespeare, but there is hope for us—for the unknowns. After all, every famous author was once an unknown.

If you want to write a book and are serious about getting it published, you must be armed with a computer, a current edition of WRITER'S MARKET (which is updated annually), and thick skin. I include *thick skin* because the stream of rejections can be devastating. One thing you must remember: A publisher is never rejecting you personally. Writing is subjective, so what may not appeal to one editor in a company may appeal to another. Also, many publishers prepare a five-year publishing plan, and your manuscript might not fit into that plan.

SO YOU WANT TO BE A WRITER!

Everyone has a story to tell or valuable information they'd like to share. Some manuscripts get published and others merely collect dust on the author's bookshelf. Not everyone becomes a household legend like Agatha Christie or James Michener, let alone William Shakespeare, but there is hope for us—for the unknowns. After all, every famous author was once an unknown.

If you want to write a book and are serious about getting it published, you must be armed with a computer, a current edition of WRITER'S MARKET (which is updated annually), and thick skin. I include *thick skin* because the stream of rejections can be devastating. One thing you must remember: A publisher is never rejecting you personally. Writing is subjective, so what may not appeal to one editor in a company may appeal to another. Also, many publishers prepare a five-year publishing plan, and your manuscript

Type this modified block letter as it appears. Supply the current date and type your initials instead of *xx*. Be certain that placement of the parts of the letter is correct and that the letter is vertically and horizontally centered.

```
                                        Date


        Mr. Eric Laurence
        23 Northeastern Avenue
        Columbia, MD 21044

        Dear Mr. Laurence:

        Re: Modified Block Style

        Modified block has traditionally been the most
        commonly used of all letter styles.

        The most noted difference between this style and the
        full block style is that the date and complimentary
        closing are slightly to the right of center. Note
        that the subject line, the inside address, and all
        paragraphs remain flush with the left margin.

        This letter style is very appealing to the eye and is
        very popular.


                                Sincerely,



                                Jon A. Roberts
        xx
```

COMMONLY MISSPELLED CITIES

Akron	OH	Memphis	TN
Albuquerque	NM	Miami	FL
Baton Rouge	LA	Milwaukee	WI
Beaumont	TX	Minneapolis	MN
Berkeley	CA	New Orleans	LA
Bridgeport	CT	Omaha	NE
Buffalo	NY	Philadelphia	PA
Chattanooga	TN	Phoenix	AZ
Chicago	IL	Pittsburgh	PA
Cincinnati	OH	Racine	WI
Cleveland	OH	Raleigh	NC
Des Moines	IA	San Francisco	CA
Detroit	MI	Savannah	GA
Duluth	MN	Seattle	WA
Gary	IN	Shreveport	LA
Honolulu	HI	Syracuse	NY
Knoxville	TN	Tucson	AZ
Lincoln	NE	Wilkes-Barre	PA
Louisville	KY	Wilmington	DE
Macon	GA	Worcester	MA

Letters and Memorandum Styles

Full Block Style

Full block is the most popular letter style. Type this full block letter as it appears. Supply the current date and type your initials instead of *xx*. Be certain that placement of the parts of the letter is correct and that the letter is vertically and horizontally centered.

```
Date

Mr. Marc Alan
345 Peachtree Place, NW
Atlanta, GA 30318

Dear Mr. Alan:

Re: Full Block Style

This easy-to-keyboard letter style is becoming
more and more popular and is widely used in many of
today's modern offices.

It is a very efficient style because everything
begins at the left margin, thereby eliminating
the need to set tabs or be concerned about whether
the date and complimentary closing are too far
to the left or right. We are now in an era where
productivity is a major concern; therefore, this
letter style will, over a period of time, increase
the flow of paperwork.

I hope you will consider using this new style as you
prepare for the office you will soon be opening.

Very truly yours,


Jon A. Roberts

xx
```

Red, White, and Blue

Type the "color expressions" corresponding to the following.

Example: livid = saw red

1. bribery

2. gabs a lot

3. cowardly

4. VIP handling

5. give the go-ahead

6. delighted

7. the focus of public attention

8. take one's lunch to work

9. conceal

10. having an unduly optimistic outlook

The answers are on page 195.

Timed Typings

```
Dear Fred:                                          2
     Please be advised that the audition scheduled  12
for Monday, December 13, has been changed. The new  22
date will be Wednesday, December 15. We will still  32
meet at 9:30 A.M. We will break for lunch at about  42
noon and will resume at one. We will also take two  52
15-minute breaks: one in the morning and the other  62
in the afternoon. If the new date should cause you  72
any problems, kindly advise me as soon as you can.  82
```

1   2   3   4   5   6   7   8   9   10
_____

```
Dear Mr. Myers:                                     3
     By now you must have heard the good news! Our  13
division has been selected as the year's recipient  23
of the Kirland International Award for Excellence.   33
This is a great honor and I personally want to thank 43
each one on the team who helped make this division  53
a success. It is people like you whom we are proud  63
to call the company's most treasured assets.        71
```

1   2   3   4   5   6   7   8   9   10
_____

Letters, Envelopes, and Memos

Letters and memos are common forms of business communication. When you are typing a letter, be concerned with the letter's organization, completeness, accuracy, clarity, and neatness. Also, center the letter vertically and horizontally, forming an imaginary frame around the text. Check the page preview on your word processor to see how your document will look when it prints. When you finish the letter, you should be proud to place your signature or reference initials on it.

Margin Guidelines

Short Letter (approximately 125 words or less)

1.5" left and right margins

3" top and bottom margins

Average Letter (approximately 126–225 words)

2.25" left and right margins

2.5" top and bottom margins

Long Letter (approximately 226 words or more)

.75"–1" left and right margins

2" top and bottom margins

Help Menu

Refer to your Help menu or user manual for the following:

- Margins
- Customized Form Letters

Parts of a Business Letter

The following explains all the parts of a letter. Please see the example on page 101 for a visual display.

Date

Always write the date in full; do not abbreviate.

Mailing or In-House Notation

Mailing notations can be Special Delivery, Certified Mail, or Registered Mail and in-house notations can be Confidential, Please Hold, etc. Each is placed two lines below the date, always at the left margin. They can be capitalized and/or underscored.

Date	April 8, 20—
Mailing or In-House Notation	CERTIFIED MAIL
Inside Address Attention Line	Marric Production Company Attention Marc N. Eric 3 Ternure Avenue Monsey, NY 10952
Salutation	Gentlemen:
Subject or Reference Line	Re: Letter of Recommendation for Kathy Wertalik
Body (Message)	It is a pleasure to write this letter of recommendation on behalf of Kathy Wertalik. She was in my employ as a part-time secretary/receptionist for five years and left to seek full-time employment with another company. Unfortunately, our company is quite small, and there were no advancement possibilities for her within our organization. I found Ms. Wertalik to be a person of high integrity who worked tirelessly and with the highest degree of efficiency. Her tact is unquestionable and her skills are top-notch. She was a most valued employee, and any company would be most fortunate to have her join its staff.
Complimentary Closing	Sincerely,
Signature Line	Jon A. Roberts
Reference Initials	pt
Enclosure Notation	Enclosure
Copy Notation	cc: Kathy Wertalik
Postscript	I have enclosed a copy of the records you requested.

Inside Address	The inside address starts four lines below the date (or two lines below the mailing or in-house notation) and includes the name of the person to whom you are writing, the name of the company, the full street address, and the city, state, and Zip Code.
Attention Line	The attention line, which is part of the inside address, is used when you are writing to a company and want the letter directed to a particular person or department. It is presented in one of the following ways:

```
ReMARCable Drafting & Design
561 Banks Street
San Francisco, CA 94110
Attention Marc A. Lindsell

ReMARCable Drafting & Design
Attention Marc A. Lindsell
561 Banks Street
San Francisco, CA 94110
```

Salutation	The salutation is placed two lines below the last line of the address and should correspond to the first line of the inside address.

```
ABC Company . . . . . . . . Ladies or Gentlemen:
Ms. Janice Teisch . . . . . . . Dear Ms. Teisch:
Personnel Director . . . . . Dear Sir or Madam:
```

Subject or Reference Line	The subject line is considered part of the letter; therefore, it should always be placed two lines below the salutation. Its purpose is to direct the reader to the theme of the letter. Horizontal placement depends on the letter style selected.
Body (Message)	The body of the letter is generally single-spaced with double-spacing between the paragraphs.

- The opening paragraph is generally short. It serves as an introduction.
- The middle paragraph(s) supports the opening. It provides additional information.
- The final paragraph is generally short. It serves as a summation, request, suggestion, or look to the future.

Complimentary Closing	The complimentary closing appears two lines below the last typewritten paragraph line. Horizontal placement depends on the letter style selected.

Letters, Envelopes, and Memos

Signature Line	Horizontal placement of the signature line depends on the letter style selected. Some variations are:

```
Very truly yours,           Very truly yours,
ROBERTS CONSULTING CO.
                            Jon A. Roberts

Jon A. Roberts
```

Reference Initials	Reference initials are used when someone other than the writer types the letter. Initials always appear at the left margin and include either the writer's and typist's initials or the typist's initials only.

```
SLR
slr
SLR/JAR
```

Enclosure Notation	The enclosure notation appears on the line below the reference initials when additional material is included with the letter. The word *Enclosure* is sufficient; however, some people list the enclosures or indicate the number of enclosures. Another option is to use the word *Attachment* for such material.

```
Enclosure
enc.
Enc. 2 (for number of enclosures)
Attachment
```

Copy Notation	When a copy of the letter is being sent to a third party, a *cc* notation (held over from the days of carbon copies) is often included. It appears directly below the enclosure notation or reference initials and is followed by the name of the person to whom the copy is being sent. The initials *pc*, for "photocopy," are often used in place of *cc*.
	In the event the writer does not want to notify the addressee that a third party will be receiving a copy, a *bc* (blind copy) or *bcc* (blind carbon copy) notation is made on the copy only.
Postscript	A postscript notation is used for emphasis. The postscript should be used sparingly because it could be interpreted as an afterthought, indicating a lack of organization on the part of the writer. A postscript is placed two lines below the last notation, with or without the P.S. notation.